MW00977335

journey

journey

One woman's decades-long journey through grief to spiritual enlightenment

DR. LYNDA BOUCUGNANI-WHITEHEAD

author
ready

For information contact:
drlyndaauthor30@gmail.com

Published by:
Author Ready

Cover design: Satori at 99designs

Interior book design:
Francine Platt, Eden Graphics, Inc. • edengraphics.net

Paperback ISBN 978-1-958626-46-7

Hardback ISBN 978-1-958626-48-1

Ebook ISBN 978-1-958626-47-4

Library of Congress Number: 2023911215

Manufactured in the United States of America

First Edition

The love between a parent and child
is the greatest gift that has been given to us.

Love is Eternal and Love is all there is.

This book is dedicated to my children

David Agustin Boucugnani

AND

Maria-Victoria Boucugnani

Coincidence
is GOD'S WAY of
staying *anonymous.*

Table of Contents

Who Might Benefit from the Messages in This Book?

Journey is designed for multiple readers.

OF COURSE, those who have sustained a profound loss may benefit by learning what this new life could be like for them. Those of us who *know,* realize that our life is now divided into the *Before and the After*, especially for those who have lost their child. Perhaps they may be comforted and informed by it.

Anyone who has suffered a profound loss may learn in these pages about finding hope, the elusive joy, and how normal they really are. Friends and family may learn how to help; what to do, what not to do, and better understand what living life in the *After* feels like for their loved one.

Additional major audiences are the professionals who are called upon to help when such a profound loss is experienced. Psychologists, school psychologists, counselors, therapists, physicians, religious professionals, and persons leading grief groups in various organizations are among those who may gain insight.

In my experience, as well as others I know in the same shoes, we recognize there is a definite shortage of professionals who know how to effectively help with compassion, an open mind, and acceptance of various viewpoints. Flexibility is an essential requirement. This book is designed for this group, as well as those learning to do this work.

I would especially love to see everyday *good people* read this book. Those who care about others and would like to be prepared when their help is needed. This includes students of all kinds.

Organizations such as *Compassionate Friends* are very dear to my heart and have already used several of the speeches and articles that are included within to assist newcomers into the "fraternity that no one really ever wants to join."

Compassionate Friends is a wonderful organization that has helped so many grieving parents, and I would like to donate as many copies of this book as possible to this organization across the country. My hope is that they may use it as an asset to continue to help others.

I believe *Compassionate Friends* literally saved my life. I'm especially indebted to Freddie and Charlotte Saye who led my local chapter and to the Tucker (Georgia) chapter as well.

I participated actively for ten years and learned what we all learned: *By helping others we help ourselves.*

Let Me Tell You a Little About Myself

.... so you might better understand where I am coming from in writing these pages.

Professionally, I am a neuropsychologist. You may be asking, "what is that?" Well, a neuropsychologist studies the brain and the interaction of the brain on behavior and learning.

I began as a school psychologist and later Director of Psychological Services, Research and Development for a midsize school system outside of Atlanta, Georgia.

After twenty-five years there, and several years after receiving my PhD, I moved into private practice in neuropsychology. This fantastic and incredibly rewarding career continued for a total of over forty-five years. I consulted for specialty schools and set up curriculum and techniques for children and young adults with various difficulties. These included autism, closed head injuries, learning disabilities of all flavors, anxiety, emotional and behavioral problems, ADHD, disease processes affecting the brain, and the effects of drugs and even chemotherapy on the developing brain.

I worked with thousands of children, their parents, their teachers, and other professionals during my career.

In a nutshell, my job as a neuropsychologist involved figuring out what was happening in a kid's brain who was experiencing these types of problems, then determining the best therapeutic and educational strategies to help them deal with it.

It was necessary to communicate to parents and teachers just how to facilitate and implement the best strategies for each child. It also required the training of teachers and other professionals in various techniques that could help children, adolescents, and young adults to navigate and succeed in the early years of their lives.

Such work involves constant, up-to-date research, requires an open mind to new theories and techniques, continuous learning, and constant revisions to develop the best practices to find what really works in each individual case. So, much of this science/orientation is reflected in my spiritual journey as well.

My experience and education suddenly became a part of my own journey.

On September 13, 1996, my beautiful daughter, Maria-Victoria Boucugnani was killed. She was an exceptionally kind and compassionate person, and smart as a whip.

Her brother was driving them home from school when her life was taken as a speeding driver in a van ran a red light.

This is the story of my own survival, my own journey through this immense grief, my incredible experiences along the way, and life altering perceptions culminating in what I believe is my personal spiritual enlightenment.

It is also, indirectly, the story of a beautiful young soul, here for only a short time but with profound effect on those she met, simply by being herself. This story is full of experiences and incidents that, I believe, are evidence to support my favorite quote of all time, Albert Einstein's famous, *Coincidence is God's way of staying anonymous.*

These *coincidences* (which are really not coincidences at all), have played a very important role in my spiritual enlightenment.

It is *my hope* that this book will provide others who are on a similar journey, with hope, peace, and comfort. I offer here some guidelines for coping with such loss, and an understanding that one must be open to all possibilities, knowing that love never dies.

– *Lynda Boucugnani-Whitehead*

Prologue

Just like there is no right or wrong way to grieve, there is no particularly right way to read this book. Some of you may prefer to read the whole thing first, then go back and look at parts that especially resonate with you. Others may want to read a chapter at a time, do some self-reflection, and maybe make notes; especially if you are a professional wishing to expand your learning about how to truly help others.

The key is do what works for you.

This book has taken over twenty-seven years to write; for a very good reason. It is unusual in many ways and has multiple purposes with different potential audiences and readers. It is a story about survival but also about the spiritual journey of one person, influenced by so many others, to a state of spiritual enlightenment that could *only* happen and be told after living it.

So, time is a major factor in its presentation. I do believe it is unusual to find a chronology of grief—what it feels like and how it is handled over intervals spanning almost three decades. How events, learning, and insights actually mold one's personality, beliefs, spiritual knowledge, and development.

Yes, it had to be lived before it could be written.

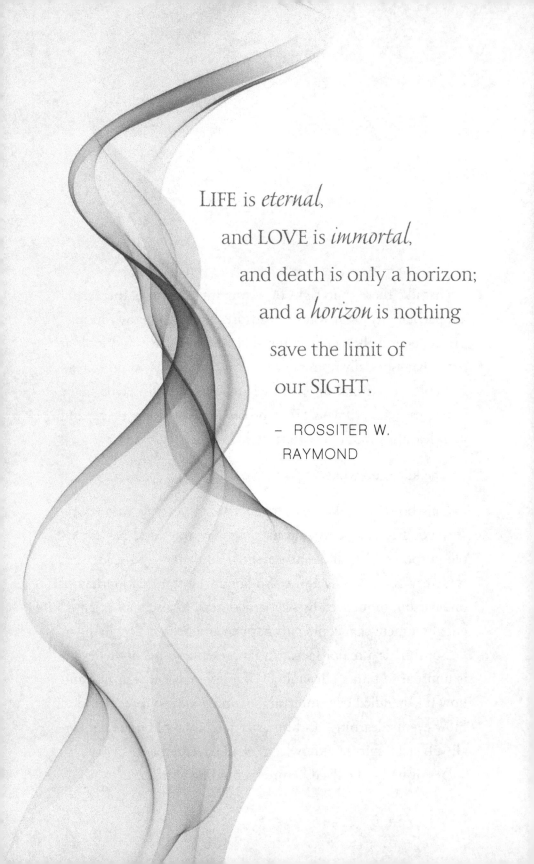

LIFE is *eternal*,

and LOVE is *immortal*,

and death is only a horizon;

and a *horizon* is nothing

save the limit of

our SIGHT.

– ROSSITER W.
RAYMOND

CHAPTER ONE

The Journey to Hope

4 Years in the After

On September 13, 1996, my daughter and I began a spiritual journey, together. Though separated physically, we were, and are, very much united in spirit. As *Compassionate Friends* we are on this soul journey together; all of us in this room, at the same time.

When we have *lost* someone we love so much, it is hard to come to terms with what this profound change means for our lives. We know in our hearts that the love we feel does not just stop. This is as incomprehensible to us as the reality of death itself. I believe that this is the first lesson I learned on my journey. *Love is not a physical thing—it is a purely spiritual presence.* Although physically, my daughter, or your son or daughter or grandchild, is not here with us, the spirit, the essence of our children is always with us.

It is a strange and disconcerting feeling to feel intense love and intense grief at the same time. We, as *Compassionate Friends,* know better than most how intense personal grief is. Surely no one could feel the enormity of grief *I feel.* I believe that no one could possibly understand this wrenching pain. Until I look into the faces of you Susan, Diane, Charlotte, Domingo, Judy, David, and all of us, who have been united in this most extraordinary way.

My own spiritual growth has been profound since embarking over four years ago on this excursion into spirit. I have replaced the questions of fresh, raw grief. Why? Why me? What if?

Now there are different questions that I will embrace as I travel up the spiritual highway. My questions now are more like:

"How do I give my love to you now, honey?"
"How do I keep our spiritual connection strong?"
"How have I grown as the result of this experience?"

This last question is of immense importance because the answer to it is the reason to continue to live. I don't pretend to know the answer, but I will continue to search for it. Have I grown as the result of this experience? Absolutely.

There is a Chinese proverb which says, "The man who moved mountains began by carrying away small stones."

So, it is with the mountain of grief.

Our spiritual journeys will all be different. We will be influenced by the various directions we take, the travelers we encounter, the ideas we embrace. There is no one map to follow, no travel agency that will guarantee a safe and hazard-free journey. I would like to share some of my own landmarks in this personal journey in the hope that some common occurrences among us will assure us that we are never alone.

My Maria-Victoria was thirteen when she returned to her first home. She was everything a mother could wish for. Beautiful, smart, silly, confident; but most importantly, incredibly caring and concerned for others. I learned a lot from my daughter, about what is important in life, about the most exquisite love that can be known as children of God—here on earth.

After September 13, my learning accelerated. I certainly would not have consciously chosen such a supersonic ride. We all know that first year is a blur; it is again a time of a paradox, of divergent feelings—intense pain coupled with profound numbness. Those two don't seem to go together, do they. Let me share some writing from my journal at two and one-half months after Maria-Victoria died.

Grief ache is an interesting thing. In the early weeks my grief ache was so physical, affecting my whole body, and so easily identifiable. I would pray for some relief from the physical pain, some opiate to take it away because it hardly left my being.

On those rare occasions when it subsided, it was usually due to a power greater than I. Like the time I simply gave a major problem at work over to God when I said, "you handle it."

I could physically feel the pain subside when I did this and was so thankful for the relief. As the weeks have gone by, the grief ache has changed in character but is always a companion. It is less full-body physical now, and I don't have to constantly pray for relief. Now it takes different guises—like characters in a play.

There's the sick feeling I get when I realize for the thousandth time that you are really gone, and I can never hold and kiss you again in this lifetime. It is the despair I feel at thinking of the years I may have to endure without you. It is the heart-grasping sob I feel at the loss of our life together. My best friend; the treasure and hope chest of our future memories.

The loss of future memories is a profound loss. It can lead to slow tears silently running down my face or bouts of anguished crying coming from deep within. It came in waves from the very beginning. Frequent, huge storm waves at first. Now my grief is more like stormy seas with periods of relative calm, but ominous clouds ever present.

We shall see how this grief ache evolves over time. There's a special morning character in this grief ache play. One who comes on stage, never missing a performance. This character comes every morning, just after the first awareness that I'm still here, to proclaim clear and loud, that my daughter is gone, yes gone.

"And don't you worry," it reminds me, "I'm such a dependable chap that I'll never fail to deliver my message to you each morning."

I am not a fan of this particular character.

This is early grief. I equate it to the beautiful songs written by Eric Clapton, after the death of his young son. Songs like "River of Tears" and "Tears from Heaven."

As I continued my journey, with my spiritual daughter at my side, the flavor of my thoughts and writings began to change. How did this happen? If I had to find one word that would capture this, it would be *hope*. I changed my perspective about what life, death, and life again is all about.

In your case, it may be different, but without hope, it is difficult to advance on this journey.

How do you find hope? Where is it hiding? How can you pull it from within yourself?

Hope began at first for me with remembrance. In the months of the first year, I would go to the cemetery and lay next to Maria-Victoria's *bit of earth*. I called it her *bit of earth* because the summer before the September she died, Maria-Victoria had been in a community theatre production of *The Secret Garden*, which meant so much to her.

Those of you familiar with this play will remember that a major premise of it is the power of the spirit of the mother and wife who had died, to instill hope and new life into the ones left behind. In this production, Maria-Victoria played a spirit. Anyway, I'd lay on our special blanket, reach out and rub the grass as if it was her hair, and write remembrances.

Before she died—when she was in the sixth grade, we had begun a mother/daughter book about the things we loved and made us happy. We called it, *The Happy Book*. We would alternate saying and writing. She wrote things like:

"Waking up in my flowery room."

"All the wrinkles on basset hounds."

"Mommy's smile."

"Christmas time."

"Arguing with Tom—friendly arguing."

"Playing Uno and winning against David and the look of defeat on David's face."

"Sunshine coming through the window."

"Doing the Happy Book with Mommy."

After she died, I began a book with her about memories of things we did that was what our love was all about. Things like:

Snuggling under the yellow comforter and watching the X files.

Dressing you up as a bag of M and M's for Halloween.

Your messages on my answering machine at work in your little girl voice telling me how much you loved me.

As you see, and as I'm sure it was with you, it is the little everyday things that are so cherished. I began cherishing her wonderful sense of humor and dramatic talent. Through this remembrance, *hope* began to enter my life, and I realized that the value of one's life is not measured by extraordinary accomplishments, but by accomplishing things with extraordinary love.

As many of us in *Compassionate Friends* can attest to, I also had communications from my daughter, both direct and symbolic. They are so valuable to my soul and too numerous to detail, but I have chosen two of them to illustrate how help comes from *hope* through those who are still with us, our loved ones.

Several months after my daughter died, I developed a roll of film that had been sitting in a camera. I didn't know what was on it and was so delighted when one of the pictures was of Maria-Victoria in her white sweater, holding me in an embrace.

A few weeks later, my former husband and Maria-Victoria's father, had an unknown roll of film at his home. When developed, he found that it included a picture of Maria-Victoria embracing him in the same way, wearing that white sweater once again.

Nearly one year later, a friend of my son David sent me some pictures he had taken with David and Maria-Victoria up in Helen, Georgia, the previous summer. One of the pictures was of Maria-Victoria embracing her brother, in the same way she had embraced her father and me.

All three of these pictures, each of her wearing the same white sweater, came after she died. Is this a coincidence? No, I don't think so.

In those pictures from David's friend was also one of Maria-Victoria's hand holding a small butterfly. I was thinking of that picture when one day I took one of Maria-Victoria to the cemetery. While driving I thought, *wouldn't it be something if a butterfly came while I am there?* But not really expecting it.

I laid the picture on our special blanket. Soon, as I watched in awe, a beautiful butterfly landed right on the picture and stayed there for several minutes. As a symbol of *hope*, I have these pictures tonight, to share them with you, my *Compassionate Friends*.

In my search to learn, through these and many other extraordinary experiences, I have come to know that my daughter, as well as your children, are fine where they are, and that our love can never, ever go away. I have come to fully understand the passage from Corinthians:

Love bears all things, believes all things, hopes all things, endures all things. Love never dies.

Like some of you, maybe not all of you of course, I talk to my daughter all the time. Recently I asked her: "Do you have a message for me, honey?"

Immediately, I had a vision in my mind of our last summer vacation up in Helen, Georgia, where we went tubing down the Chattahoochee. The words that came to me were a direct mirror to that actual experience of tubing the river. I believe she said these words to me, and I believe these words have meaning for you as well.

She said, "We are going down this journey together. We started together. There were rough spots and joy. We glided over the water and rocks. We held hands. We were separated for a time and missed each other. You needed to go over a scary waterfall on your own. You needed help, and you got it. You were proud of taking the chance and facing the fear. Though we didn't see each other for a while, you knew I was there and coming. Then we saw each other and were reunited. We got on the bus for the return journey side by side."

This is my personal message of *hope* from my daughter.

Hope takes hold and guides us through our personal journey toward spiritual growth.

Now, I return to the questions I posed at the beginning of this talk. Let me share what I have learned so far. Remember, our ways of learning, of finding hope and peace, will all be different.

There is no best itinerary, no favored airline, no universal travel plan. I am sharing what I have learned and how I have grown from this experience:

- There is a shared destination for us all, one of hope, peace, and embracing the eternal love we share with our sons and daughters.

- I have learned that there is no way out, only a way forward.

- I have learned that where there is great love, there are always miracles.

- I have learned that if you believe that life is worth living, your belief will help create the fact.

- I have learned that our children are the greatest gift that can be given to us. That through them we have known, and will always know, the most exquisite love as children of God, the eternal love between parent and child.

I would like to share a funny story. Several weeks ago, I went to the mountains with our women's book club, for a sleepover excursion. We, of course, went shopping, and I found a wonderful indoor wind chime that is solar powered. It absorbs energy from light, and every once in a while, the mechanism will turn and make the chime go off. I brought it home and put it next to a sunny window, but I forgot to tell my husband Tom about the chime.

The next day, I got up before him and was down in the office when all of a sudden, Tom came bounding down the stairs saying, "You're not going to believe this—that chime is going off all by itself—it must be Maria-Victoria."

I laughed and told him, "Well, it may be Maria-Victoria, but it's a solar powered chime, and it's the light that makes it go off."

Weeks later, I was down in my office finishing this talk at about 11:00 at night. I went upstairs so I could read it to Tom and get his input. It had been dark for over five hours, and that chime had not made a sound that entire time. Just at this place in my talk, that chime went off, all by itself. There was no *visible* light present. Both Tom and I were tremendously affected by this. Knowing Maria-Victoria's sense of humor, as well as her caring for others, I believe this last part is a special message for us all from our children.

So, at this special Christmas season, let us remember the love and smiles of our children, their delight in the wonders of the season and especially—joy.

I'd like to close with a few lyrics from "Bit of Earth" from *The Secret Garden.*

A bit of earth
A drop of dew, a single stem
Begins to rise.
That bit of earth
Is pushed away, the flowers bloom,
Before our eyes
For in the earth
A charm's at work
The word is passed,
The days are warm.
Unfold and grow,
The winter's past
We're free from harm.

From a talk given to Compassionate Friends, Jonesboro Chapter, Christmas Candle lighting Service. December 4, 2000, by Lynda Boucugnani-Whitehead in honor of her daughter, Maria-Victoria Boucugnani, and all of our children.

BACK FROM THE FUTURE

It is difficult and rather unnerving to reflect back from the future to the first early years of raw, all-consuming grief.

I remember that I can't remember; the word "blur" is very appropriate. There are tidbits of visual remembrances and feelings in this early life in the *After* that are only partially connected to reality. I was often too numb to know where I was.

I remember long periods of drift without joy and constant questions aimed at both God and me; what am I supposed to do now?

Then there were periods of intensity—things I had to do—that were so important to me: making sure Maria-Victoria was remembered and taking care of my son, David, who lost his very best friend. Now, without his only sibling.

David was dealing with his own horrendous grief aches, especially survivor's guilt. Biggest of all was trying to find the elusive "hope" that would allow me to live.

Yes, there were times when I would truly think about positioning my car so that it would be hit as I tried to cross an intersection. I don't think that's unusual. I would have to jerk myself back from that thought, usually, by thinking about how this would affect my son and other family members or hurt innocent people. It is a thought, though, that is contemplated, and in some cases, acted upon by compassionate friends.

In the early years, I spent a lot of time at the cemetery somehow thinking that it was there that I would be closest to Maria-Victoria. That changed rather dramatically over the years. Now, I really don't want to go there and only go when I want to change her flower arrangement or put up a special tribute on her birthday. This is perfectly normal folks. She is not there, she is everywhere.

I believe that finding HOPE was my first key for this spiritual journey. Hope is personal. I can't tell you how to find it, I can only tell you what worked for me.

I read over two-hundred books on death, what happens to us after we die, near-death experiences, communication with our departed loved ones, survival of consciousness, various religious perspectives on life after death, and revisited my own religious upbringing; all with a very open mind. The second major key for the spiritual journey is: learning to PAY ATTENTION. So much occurs that tells us we're on the right track, but if we're not attuned to paying attention and being alert to validation of our beliefs, we will miss them.

To make it through the travails of such profound loss, such enormous grief, one chooses one's own path. I believe the journey is helped immensely when you:

- Realize that love is spiritual, endless, and that love is all there is.

- Find your personal hope.

- Approach life with an open mind and the desire to learn and gain knowledge.

- Pay attention.

SUFFERING

has been *stronger*

than all other teaching

and has *taught me to*

understand what your heart

used to be. I have been

BENT and BROKEN, but—

I hope—into a better shape.

– CHARLES DICKENS

CHAPTER TWO

A Grief Shared

5 Years in the After

This will not be the typical article you often see in a professional publication. There will be no references to scholarly works, no discussion of what has been gleaned from years of research, no statistics, no methodology. Rather, this will be a story from my heart, one that I hope may help psychologists first understand, and then do what they do best. I had the inspiration to write this article just a week or so before the tragedy in New York. In my frame of reference, following the horror at the World Trade Center and Pentagon and in Pennsylvania, perhaps this is divine inspiration. This is something I must do.

What is it like to live through such a profound grief, to have your whole life changed in an instant, to have much of your future taken away, and to find yourself in a world that you don't recognize? As Americans, we have all had at least a taste of this. Our lives have been forever changed by these events. There is a loss of a sense of security and for what the future would now be.

But what about those people who have sustained a more profound and excruciating loss—the loss of a loved one who was treasured and so much a part of the fabric of your very life. What is it like to have that person taken away so abruptly, to one minute have that loved one beside you as a part of your dream, and the next to have that person ripped away from you? What do psychologists and other helping professionals need to know in order to help those who have sustained such a loss?

This story is very personal for me and, therefore, somewhat difficult to tell. My daughter, Maria-Victoria was thirteen years old when she was killed instantly just three blocks from our home. It was a normal day, bright and sunshiny, and my life was going along as normal.

My daughter was a beautiful, intelligent, and accomplished person known for her extraordinary kindness and compassion for others. She was innocence and pure love blossoming into a leader of others and was building the confidence that could have taken her very, very far in this life.

In one second, she was here, the next second, she was not. The fifth anniversary of her death was just two days after the New York tragedy.

Within a few months of her passing, I joined a group called *Compassionate Friends*, which is a self-help group for parents who have lost children. It was a very good move. It is said that the most profound loss a person can have is the loss of a child. I can tell you that this is the truth. However, for those who have not lost children, the most profound loss is the one they have experienced or are experiencing at the present time.

Those of us in this group frequently lament about how ill-equipped others who have not experienced such pain and grief are in dealing with it as they attempt to help those who mourn the loss of a loved one.

Ministers are often the focus of such discussions, for example, and we have often wondered how we can let others, especially professionals, know what we are really experiencing in our lives. What helps and sometimes, even more importantly, what doesn't help.

This is the purpose of this story, to share with my fellow psychologists some things that in the future may enable them to be of more help. It is based on not only my own personal experiences, but those of the numerous *Compassionate Friends* who have come into my life.

You have all heard or read about the stages of grief. The work that was done in this area by pioneers such as Elizabeth Kubler-Ross is very valuable in understanding the emotions of grief. Some professionals may feel that they can help people with grief because they have studied these stages and know the sequence by heart. *Throw it all away.* People who have sustained profound loss do not want to hear about the stages of grief, it is almost an insult. They do want to know that what they are feeling is normal, that they are not crazy, that others have felt or experienced the same things. There is no sequence of grief. It is a constant, evolving journey with many diversions into emotional peaks and valleys along the way. It is a journey, and it is *never* over.

It is true that at the time of the event you are in a state of shock and numbness. In my case after a telephone call, I made my way to the accident site. It was eerily quiet with cars backed up in four different directions at the intersection, so that I had to drive on the wrong side of the road to get there. When I got to the scene, I was no longer within myself, I must have dissociated. I felt like I was observing everything as if I was in a movie. The people in all the cars were watching me. I imagined they were saying *that's the mother.*

I was aware that I was playing this *role.*

I imagine that many of the relatives looking for loved ones in New York must have felt this way too.

At the hospital, I was placed in a special room meant to be a comfort but cut off from others. It did allow me to get out of the movie.

What helped? Friends coming to be with me. You need to hold and touch people. You need them to hold you and just be there for you.

What didn't help? Waiting a full one and one half hours to be told whether my children were alive or dead. I already knew in my heart and soul that Maria-Victoria was gone from this life, but to have a doctor finally come in and say in a cool and dispassionate manner "your daughter is deceased," made me angry.

A simple "I'm so sorry," a touch on the hand, and some semblance of compassion would have endeared this doctor to me for life. Why is that so hard to do?

We are blessed with this state of shock that comes almost immediately after suffering a traumatic loss. It allows us to do the things we have to do. For many of us, this is very, very important. I needed to make sure that Maria-Victoria had a wonderful, up-lifting funeral service that told the world about the wonderfulness of my little girl. I needed to write an obituary that would touch the hearts of Atlanta. I needed to comfort her teachers and students at her school, thereby comforting myself. I needed to be there for the hundreds of people who came to show they cared. Some people criticized the news coverage in New York of friends and relatives showing flyers of their missing loved ones saying it was exploitation. I spoke at them through my TV set. "You just don't get it. They need to do this. They have to let others know about the one they love. They need to feel like they are doing something to take care of those that are lost."

What helped me so much in the initial weeks after the accident were touches from the hearts of other people. I savored all the cards, the incredible amount of food from individuals and whole schools, letters, and phone calls from people I had never met who were touched by my daughter's story, and the physical presence of people I was close to. Such heartfelt gestures give life when life has gone out of your existence.

There is a time when you must go back to work and start to live this new life. I was fortunate to have such a wonderful, supportive staff that literally carried me through that first year. Others are not so fortunate. Some have to go back to work just days after the funeral and are expected to perform as if nothing has happened. When a traumatic loss has struck your life, you are amazed and perhaps a little bit angry that the world has gone on.

You ask yourself, "How can these normal things still go on? How can people laugh? Don't they know the world has ended?"

You think that you will never laugh again, that you will never feel joy again. In fact, it is incomprehensible to imagine that you could.

During that first year (time will vary among folks) you are literally *out of your mind*. Believe it or not, there is actually a *physical pain*, usually in your heart and chest area, but all through your body at times. This pain is experienced by many and is so excruciating you think it will never go away. Mine lasted about two months, and then it just floated away.

It was a relief to say goodbye to that constant companion. You are *out of your mind* because you think about your loved one constantly. It certainly seems a million times a day. That doesn't leave much room for concentration or memory of anything else.

Those who have experienced such loss should know that this is perfectly normal. It is perfectly normal to put the iron in the refrigerator. At work, if you don't have support, you will most likely not be able to function like you used to. You may be able to do some things on automatic pilot, but this is not the time to be making major decisions, and you, and the business you work for, must give you leeway for your memory lapses and perhaps loss of drive.

Every day is a struggle just to get up and live, and each day you do is an accomplishment. So be supportive and tolerant. Make it a point to know about these cognitive disturbances, assist the person you are helping to understand them. And if you are in a position to do so, make their employers aware, know what to expect, and how to give support.

There is no timetable for grief. It is highly offensive to the grief-stricken to hear things like, "you need to move on." Or to receive messages that you are expected to be back to normal and "over it" in a certain time frame.

A principal came up to me about three months after Maria-Victoria died and said, "Well, have you gotten over the death of your lovely daughter?" I swear this is true. My response was, rather curtly, "I will *never* get over it."

This kind-hearted man had no clue about how much that remark hurt. Let me tell you that you never get over it. You are changed. A different person from the one you were before the death of your loved one. Besides, we don't want to get over it because that suggests that we can somehow let that love go.

That brings me to the dreaded *C* word. A word hated by the bereaved, and one especially pertinent to those people who have loved ones missing in New York. The dreaded C word is *closure*. I hate that word. I am offended by that word. Most of the bereaved I know hate it too. There is no such thing as closure. You never get over it and quit expecting us to. People must learn to say something else. Something like *relief from uncertainty* is more like it.

There is usually a lot of support and attention paid to the bereaved at the time of the loss and for a short time afterward. But after a while that support fades and contacts drop off. Many, if not all, of my *Compassionate Friends* report that this is a time when you know who your real friends are. Sometimes people don't know what to say, and so they avoid you. Especially in cases where children have died, people avoid you because they think it might be "contagious." If this most horrendous of nightmares happens to you, it could happen to me. I don't want to think about that, so I'll stay away from you. You may be shaking your head in disbelief, but it is true. Many find that family members are the least helpful. They do not want to bring it up because they think it will cause you pain, but it is more about their pain.

If you remember one thing from this story, remember what is in this paragraph. The most precious words a person who has lost a loved one can hear are their loved one's name. Say it over and over again. It will not bring pain; it has great potential to bring joy and to heal. *MARIA-VICTORIA, MARIA-VIC-TORIA.* Hearing her name always lightens my heart. In the beginning, people need to tell their story, repeatedly. Your job is to listen, to give a hug, or show that you feel for them. It was important for those missing loved ones in New York or for those who knew their loved one had died, to "tell their story." This is a part of the grief process, and a way to validate the strength of their continuing love for their loved one. It is a way to honor them and, most importantly, to assure that they will not be forgotten. That is the greatest fear of those of us who have lost our children, and probably for other bereaved persons as well. We do not want our loved ones to be forgotten. You are doing the bereaved a wonderful favor when you bring up their loved one's name and when you reminisce about something that they did or something special about them. It is a very, very special gift and so easy to give.

There can come a time when the bereaved person starts to refrain from bringing up their loved one's name or talking about them because they are afraid of making the other person uncomfortable. A lot of people don't know what to say, and so they say nothing. You quickly learn who you can trust and who you can't to spill your heart to. People are afraid that what they might say will sound awkward or mistakenly think it will bring pain. This then can be misinterpreted by the bereaved person as a sign that you don't care. Never say, "I know just how you feel," because you don't, you have no idea. Never say, "I don't know how you do it. If it were me, I'd just die." My goodness, that implies that I must not have loved my child enough because I didn't die.

So, what helps? A heartfelt hug or saying, "I think about you often." Or maybe, "I was thinking about Maria-Victoria today." "I know this is a hard time for you." "I am so sorry."

I went to see a therapist for about a year after Maria-Victoria died. What I liked about her the most was that she told me at the beginning that she knew very little about dealing with grief but felt that she was going to learn a lot by our time together. She did learn a lot, and I got a chance to tell my story, to process how my life had changed, and to run through ideas about how to redefine my life and redefine my relationship with my daughter. In essence, in the long term that is what we, as psychologists, need to do to help others. When you have experienced a traumatic loss, you must make a choice. You choose whether to retreat from life, to give up on life and what you held dear, or to grow from this horrendous experience. Making this choice is not easy, but it is a choice. You also must redefine your relationship with your loved one. You may not have a physical relationship anymore, but you can choose to always have a strong and loving relationship. My feeling of connectedness with my daughter is very, very strong. She is very much a part of my life and will always be. I have redefined my relationship with her and do the things I want and need to do to keep our love and connection alive.

As you go on this grief journey, do whatever feels right to you. There are no rules. In the beginning, I would go to the cemetery and lay on a blanket and stroke the grass over her grave as if it was her hair. Imagine the sight of that to one that does not know. I still, after five years, have not washed the clothes from her clothes hamper. I probably never will.

Before I moved, I would go into her bedroom at night, smell her sheets, or sleep in her bed. I talk to her aloud every day. These are all perfectly normal things to do. As a psychologist, it is important to validate to the bereaved person that *anything* they want to do that brings them comfort is okay. We all have different ways of grieving, and we all need to respect these different ways.

I am a very different person from the one I was before my daughter died. I think I'm a better person. A lot of my friends think so too. What can come out of tragedy is growth, often spiritual. Everyone I know in *Compassionate Friends*, including me, no longer have any fear of death.

Death is the door to where my daughter is. When fear is gone, because the worst that could happen, has already happened, it is a very freeing experience. You are less afraid of change, you are less tolerant of arrogant, insensitive people or of doing things that don't have meaning for you anymore. You put your energy toward the things that are truly meaningful in this world. That doesn't mean you don't go through periods of sadness and despair and have to pull yourself up time and again, of course, you do, but you are not necessarily suffering from depression, but *profound sadness*, and there is a difference.

When you are depressed, you don't want to do anything, and you don't grow. When you are experiencing profound sadness, you still want to grow, to do things that will make a difference; you often feel compelled to do so.

As psychologists, and as friends or colleagues of those who have experienced a traumatic loss, we can help by supporting them on their own personal journeys, not by telling them where and when to go, but by being a friendly landmark along the way. We help by realizing there is no destination, not even an itinerary. At five years after my daughter's death, I probably think about my daughter about five hundred times a day, rather than a million. Some would call that progress. I call it evolution.

A few days ago, after putting flowers and five heart balloons on my daughter's grave, I found a card and letter left there by one of her friends. What a gift to me and my daughter. I close this story with her words so that we can all remember what really matters.

> *I thought I saw you dancing,*
> *but it was only the leaves in the wind.*
> *I thought I heard you laughing,*
> *but it was only the waves of the sea.*
> *I thought I felt you touch me,*
> *but it was only a moonlit dream…*
> *but I know I felt you in my heart,*
> *because I miss you very much.*
> *I love you.*

I met a girl about a year ago who when I first saw her,
I thought it was you. I had to take a double glance and
every time since then, when I see her from a distance or run
into her, I always think I see you! She favors you so much
in appearance but I'm sure she could never be as loving,
good-hearted, and caring as you were. The angel ornament
reminds me of you, always caring and watching out for others!
Miss you more and more each day!
Friends Forever.
Love Always,
Kristen

BACK FROM THE FUTURE

This is a very special picture to me. This was at the seventh grade honors program at Maria-Victoria's school with some of her teachers as she was receiving the Super Star Student of the Year Award, the highest award one could receive. Wow—was I proud! Maria-Victoria and I had so much fun picking out her white outfit. White was her favorite color—and it was mine too, it still is. A few months later, she was buried in this outfit along with her white bear. She had to go up and receive so many awards at this assembly, and I know she felt so good dressed as she was. I'd call it sophisticated.

I mentioned that both Maria-Victoria and I had premonitions of something that was going to happen for about eight months before the accident that took her life.

Initially, I thought it was going to be me, but it rapidly switched to something happening to one of my children. Then it was David. He had won so many awards in science in his last year in high school. For one such award he had to fly across the country to receive an award for inventing a procedure that measured the error when scientists measuring the length of DNA strands reuse the same gel or viewing medium. He then developed a formula to compensate for the error, saving thousands of dollars for each procedure. So, David won trips to San Diego, Tucson, and West Virginia. He was traveling a lot. I was so scared.

It was about this time that Maria-Victoria began to display some unusual behavior. Although she was mostly her normal self, on the Mother's Day before she died, she had rooted out all of the Mother's Day cards she had *ever* given me and had them all laid out on the kitchen table along with her new card and gift. If you are not paying attention, you may fail to see the significance of this, but I certainly did, in retrospect.

After she died, I found a note she had written to her teacher Mr. B. The wording of it also struck me as unusual and meaningful.

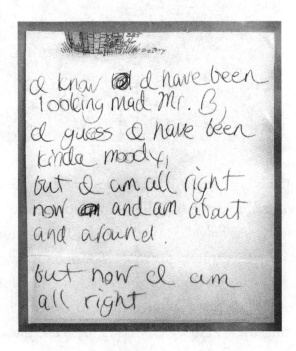

I came across a more lengthy version she had written than this scribbled note that said:

I know I have been looking mad Mr. B,
I guess I have been kinda moody.
I understand why you ask what's wrong,
Because that is part of your duty.
I am alright now and thanks for being so kind,
I am going to miss you,
I am alright now.
And about the questions, I don't mind,
I am going to miss you.
You are surely one-of-a-kind.
Alright truly.

Perhaps another premonition not long before she left us, but I zeroed in on the words "but I am all right now and about and around but now I am all right." Coming back from the future I *know*; she is about and around.

Mr. B spoke at her funeral.

Maria-Victoria was in a production of *The Secret Garden* in August 1996, just before her death in September. I remember going to the auditions and hugging her and holding her hand as she went through each stage of the process. This was the first time she had ever auditioned for a production. I kept thinking, *I don't think I could ever do something like this.* It required such focus and maturity. She handled it beautifully, and I got a glimpse of the incredible talent she had. Of course, mother and daughter hoped for the main role of Mary, but we were realistic that there were others much more seasoned auditioning for the play, and that it would be quite unlikely.

This play is about the spiritual connection of a mother for her daughter, after the mother passes away and the communication between them and the messages sent. It is a beautiful play with gorgeous music. Well, lo and behold, Maria-Victoria got the role of a *spirit* and was the understudy for the role of Mary. I so loved that she got this opportunity, and yes, I paid attention to the fact that she played the role of a spirit in a play steeped in communication between the two worlds. Remember, *coincidence is God's way of staying anonymous.*

Clayton Alliance for Summer Theater
The Secret Garden

*Picture Time
Photography*

Maria-Victoria is in the first row, third from left – all in white.

During that last summer together, one of my favorite memories is of Maria-Victoria laying on my bed with me and listening to and singing along to the songs of *The Secret Garden* and practicing her lines. It was heaven. We had talked about what we thought heaven would be like, sort of designing it for ourselves, certainly assuming that we would be there together. Our heaven where we spent most of our time was all white, but with vibrant shots of color all over the place in the form of flowers, trees galore, and art. The contrast of the white with such color was mesmerizing. Our heaven had lots and lots of music and singing. It was beyond description in human words.

About two years after she died, I went to see the movie, *What Dreams May Come* starring Robin Williams. The COLOR in heaven I am talking about was exemplified beautifully in this movie, like sloshy paint you could walk on and sink into. I must tell you I am an extremely empathetic and intuitive person, and I live other people's feelings. The gorgeous ending of this movie almost did me in, but with luck, I was with some of my anchors and lifesaver girlfriends who held me up. I just sobbed uncontrollably, good sob, and couldn't seem to stop. I couldn't really breathe.

The only other time I had uncontrollable sobbing in a movie theater was while watching *Schindler's List* with Maria-Victoria and David. However, that was a sad sob, and was much worse and debilitating. My kids weren't embarrassed by their Mom's behavior. They understood.

As the last summer progressed, Maria-Victoria seemed uneasy and out of character a little. My independent girl had difficulty sleeping and would sometimes ask me to sleep with her, and I did. She seemed worried and a little out of sorts, as exemplified by her note to Mr. B. She was a little on the anxious side. She wanted her big white bear to be with her in her bed. And she wanted me.

That was also the summer of the bombing at the Olympics in Atlanta. We went to see the memorial and all the flowers and little flags in remembrance of those who had died or were injured. But it didn't overtake her life. She was often happy and so excited about eighth grade where she had just been elected President of the Beta Club. I believe she had her first possibility of a boyfriend, and he was really cute!

There are three
NEEDS of the griever:
To *find the words* for
the loss, to *say* the words
aloud and to *know*
that the words
have been heard.

– VICTORIA ALEXANDER

CHAPTER THREE

Please Understand - Please Comfort Us

"A Grief Shared" was first published in a magazine called *The Dialogue* put out by the Georgia Association of School Psychologists. However, it quickly spread all over the country with other State School Psychology organizations. It was also published in the National and State *Compassionate Friends* publications and circulated around the country again. And then there was the internet. It was posted by people I didn't even know, and before you knew it, I was receiving emails from all over the country from folks who had read it and were affected by it. This was when the first seed of this book began. I would like to share a few of the many emails I received.

I want to thank you for your wonderful article in the *GASP Dialogue*. I read it with great interest since I work so frequently with families who have lost loved ones.

Your thoughtful and insightful writing really conveyed the difficulty and true heartache of this type of loss.

I have shared your article with several families, and they thanked me VERY MUCH for the helpful information. Thanks for putting your experience into words...your actions have helped others!   – John P. PhD

––––––––––––

This article is going to help more people than you will ever know. Thank you for having the courage to write it. – Beth S.

––––––––––––

Hi – I just finished reading your article in the *Dialogue of GASP*. Your words touched me and definitely made an impact on me...I admire your being able to write about this subject so openly and honestly. – Kristy G and Amy H.

––––––––––––

I wanted to touch base with you to tell you how "right on" I think your article was. My husband and I lost our first born, a son, six plus years ago and I related to all that you said. I sent your article on to friends who lost their seventeen-year-old son about 15 months ago. I know that they too will relate. Thanks for writing it!
– Judith V.

––––––––––––

This one is not an email but handwritten on yellow paper:

I voice my thanks again for your wonderful paper on grief and for your phone call. Your words have been redemptive in my personal grief. My son and I went to the gravesite April 18, one year. We placed the balloons and I 'let me go.' We watched it sail into the beauty of God's sky. One of my friends wrote, 'I made copies and sent to my pastor who is completing his doctoral studies on developing a program for his church on Grief Recovery. Thank you from the bottom of my heart.   – Earl S.

———————————

I read with wet eyes the touching account of the grief you suffered and still suffer at the loss of your daughter. It's the kind of article I would feel comfortable giving to someone who has gone through what you have endured. Thank you so much for sharing your grief with us and allowing us a glimpse into what a heartbroken parent experiences and how to help that parent grieve. Perhaps the very process of writing the article and sharing your grief with others will bring an even greater measure of comfort to you. I pray so.   – Beverly O. PhD.

———————————

I cried when I read your article. Thank you for sharing your pain and courage. Last week a friend lost her husband suddenly of heart attack, and I have been wondering and praying about what I can say to her the next time

I saw her. I hugged her at the service, couldn't think of anything to say to her that hadn't already been said by everyone else, but just told her how much we love her. I know there's nothing we can say, but I just wanted her to feel my love and support. The hard part for me will be in the coming weeks and months as we see each other weekly; as you said we who haven't experienced it are uncomfortable bringing up the subject, and uncomfortable ignoring it, like the elephant in the room. Your insight helped me understand it doesn't matter, just be there for her. I hope to share your article with the pre-school teachers she works with every day, to help them help her. I pray for you and your family in your continued journey. Thank you for sharing your heart. – Kimberly H.

Lynda, I wanted to thank you for the article you wrote for the Autumn Dialogue. The insight you provided was priceless and you were very generous in sharing your most private feelings with your colleagues. I feel I have learned a great deal about the grieving process from the experiences you shared. I lost a brother 10 years ago, and too, will never get over it. As tough as it was for my siblings and me, it was devastating for my parents. I wish I would have been better prepared to help them at that time. Your article will help many in understanding and dealing with such a loss. I know Maria-Victoria will always be with you.   – Danny S.

Lynda, just read your article last night and have thought of almost nothing else since. I found it to be one of the most profound and moving things that I've ever read. Thank you.   – Cathy M.

———————

I wanted to thank you for writing "A Grief Shared". I lost my very special daughter, Cam, almost two years ago at age 24. You wrote my deepest thoughts and feelings almost as if I had dictated them to you. She was an only child and as you wrote, we grieve not only for her but for the future—the grandchildren we will never know. In one second, I lost my precious child and my best friend; my life changed forever. The world shifted and nothing will ever be the same again. My husband and I have found that our priorities have changed and things that would have worried us or depressed do not matter anymore. My husband said the exact words you wrote—The worst thing that could happen has already happened; we have nothing to fear. Although I sobbed as I read your article, it is good to know that our reactions to the collapse of our world are shared by others in similar situations. – Angela R.

———————

I just want to thank you for your willingness to share the story of your grief journey with us. ...I plan to save this issue and refer to it again as I deal with the children in my schools and also with friends who are in similar circumstances. I also want to share it with a prayer group that I am a part of and with our system's counselors and administrators. Thank you again for using your experience to hopefully help us all to be a better support system for those we serve. May God use your daughter's life to remind others of His goodness.   – Tracy B.

––––––––––

Just wanted to say thank you for sharing your journey in the *GASP Dialogue* this month. It brought tears to my eyes as I read it. Just wanted to let you know that your story touched me deeply and that I have taken your advice to heart. It will definitely influence how I respond to people who are grieving in the future.   – Pilar M.

––––––––––

I read your article with both sadness for your loss and with respect for the excellent way in which you communicated the needs and emotions of those who have suffered a loss of this kind. I am the newsletter editor for the Colorado Society of School Psychologists, also a past President of CSSP and the former school psychologist at Columbine High School. Currently I am also involved with the Crisis Response Team which CSSP has formed and sponsored for our state. All of this leads to my request to reprint your article in our soon to be published newsletter. I would like to sincerely thank you for sharing this very poignant experience with others.   – Marilou M.

––––––––––

Note: Shortly after Columbine I was given the task of setting up the Crisis Response Intervention Program for the school system I worked for and training all personnel. As part of my research and development for doing this, I went to Washington D.C. and completed a 40 hour course to be a part of the National Community Crisis Response Team—the first of its kind. This training was invaluable and was the beginning of very extensive training in crisis response throughout our country. February 14 –18, 2000.   – Lynda

---

Lynda, I wanted to let you know how much the article you wrote has meant to two support groups in the Statesboro area. Last spring a 16 year old boy in my church was killed in a single car accident. His mother is a very private person and it has been very hard for me to know what to say to her or how to help her with her horrendous loss. Right before Christmas I sent your article to her in the mail with a short note. Several weeks later she called to tell me that the article had helped her and that she had shared it with the support group that she attends monthly. The group is made up of parents who have experienced the death of a child. My friend said that everyone in the group was amazed by what you had written. You were able to put down on paper what they experience on a daily basis. The group leader who also lost a son many years ago in an accident wanted to know where the article originated. She then took the article to a group that meets in a neighboring county. They agreed with me that you had done a wonderful thing by sharing your feelings about Maria-Victoria's life and death. They felt like I did that you should write a book. I can assure you that your article helped me talk more freely with my friend. Your daughter's life has touched many people in southeast Georgia and around the State. I hope that thought will bring some comfort to you. – Doty D.

––––––––––

After several reprintings of "A Grief Shared" in the Atlanta area Compassionate Friends newsletter, one of the responses from a parent that was sent to me:

I have been reading Dr. Lynda Boucugnani-Whitehead's article over and over and over... Somehow it comforts me to know that I am not losing my mind. It helps me to realize that I'm not alone, even though many times I think I am, but the cruel fact is there are many of us who are suffering. I started counseling yesterday to some-how help me cope with the death of my daughter, Julie, on February 25. As Lynda writes, "we never will be the same person that we were before our loss, but some-how we need to move forward, to regain our purpose in life." In my situation, I am looking for who I am now. My purpose is gone now and so now I need to move forward and find my role in life again. I wanted to let Lynda know that her article meant so much to me. I too kept Julie's clothes and have the need to smell them. Only us as parents know of that need. I am like Lynda; I love hearing Julie's name. It is perhaps the best pres-ent I could receive from someone. That they have not forgotten her. She once said to me, "mom, we will never grow old together. I guess she was right for now I grow old alone and without her. Thank you Lynda for saying what all of us think. For helping us cope and for showing us that there is a way to go on with our lives.   – Rita

_____

September 16, 1996

Dear Mrs. Whitehead,

I was literally moved to tears when I read the obituary of your precious daughter. Maria-Victoria must have been the most special of God's children and I appreciate your sharing her life with the people of Atlanta through this moving tribute to her. Now we too, those who never knew her, can thank God for her life and look toward the day when we all meet. You have my prayers through this pain. Sincerely – Molly G.

_____

April 16, 2003

Lynda, I hope this email reaches you. My granddaughter, Victoria Grace, two years, was killed on December 25, 2002. My daughter and I received great comfort from your article, "A Grief Shared". It was given to us by a very understanding and kind friend who lost her son 6 years ago. I just wanted to let you know how you touched our lives. Maria-Victoria sounds like she was a wonderful young lady who touched some lives herself. Thank You. – Nina H.

September 13, 2002

Dear Lynda, I got in too late to call you, but in case you're in front of your computer screen I wanted to tell you that I'm thinking of you on this day of such intense ambivalent feelings. I know that I will never think of September 13th the same again either Friday or not. September 11th could not displace it but was merely added to it. I have the most beautiful visual images of your precious daughter, the biggest umbrella I have seen children try to open and carry when I was coming to your home to work on our state project and it was raining. Their smiles and laughter, utter delight at the enormity of the task were completely captivating to me as I watched them approach my car. They were so proud of themselves! The essence of what we love about children, the essence of what we love about being parents. Thank you for those memories. I don't think I have talked to you since your message was published In the *Dialogue*, at least not for more than a minute or two at Spring conference. Lynda, I can't tell you what an epiphany of parental truth that was, on a subject very few would dare to bear their raw emotions on. I feel that you have done a great service to probably many more than you will ever be aware of. In fact, I would like to ask your permission to share with the group that I was asked to serve on, the steering committee with the Suicide Prevention Action Network.... I would like to be able to share your "A Grief Shared" message with each of them, so that they might benefit from your incomparable, forthcoming descriptions of your feelings, described in a way that simply makes time stand still. I have to think that the warm, forever wounded people on this committee would find a personal connectedness with your thoughts and feelings that are so perfectly expressed. Tears well up in my eyes every time I think of your words. Lynda, I am so glad I got to share the joy of your children the times that I did. It was a privilege to me and one that I treasure. It will remain permanently that way. You are very special to me, and I am just one of many who can say that. If we could thank you enough for everything that you have given and continue to give you would grow weary of it. You gave them parts of your heart that no one would ever wish to be pulling from. You will always have my admiration and love, gratefulness, and respect. It takes a strong, uncommon person to experience what you have and still be able to enrich others in multiple ways. It can't be easy. I know that the hurt will always be there. The beauty will always be there, too, and that's what I cherish. – Frank S. (Buz)

Note from Lynda: I chose some of these emails and letters to give you a flavor for how others, especially those who have lost a child, are hungry for comfort and for understanding of how it feels to go through this grief journey. I believe it also illustrates how needed information can spread very rapidly over near and far with the potential for helping as many people as possible.

I also want to emphasize how much these responses meant to me. It comforts my heart to feel that I may be helping others with the worst thing that could ever happen to them. This was the beginning inclination for my desire to write this book.

In the *universe*,
there are things that
are KNOWN, and things
that are UNKNOWN,
and *in between*, there
are DOORS.

– WILLIAM BLAKE

CHAPTER FOUR

The Permanence of Love

7 Years in the After

When I was preparing for what I wanted to say in this talk, I read over many things I had written before, including journal entries starting shortly after my daughter, Maria-Victoria's death, and other things I had written as I continued along the path. What hit me the most as I was doing this?

First was the incredible depth of the up and down feelings. On one entry I would be positive, felt spiritually connected to Maria-Victoria and even designed our own heaven. On the next I was at the depth of despair with merged feelings of hopelessness, resentment, and total shut-down.

How our lives have changed since the death of our child. Would we ever have thought that we would daily ponder the mysteries of life and of love at this depth? Yet this is a part of our new normal.

Can you even imagine your life before your child died? I find that very hard to do because this new life, with all that comes with it, has taken over who I am. I am betting you feel the same. I learned early on two very important things as I struggled to survive.

First, that I had to redefine my life and redefine my relationship with my daughter. And second, that I had to make a choice.

When you have experienced a traumatic loss, you have to make a choice. You choose whether to retreat from life, to give up on life and what you held dear, or to grow from this horrendous experience. Making this choice is not easy, but it *is a choice*.

You also must redefine your relationship with your loved one. You may not have a physical relationship anymore, but you can choose to always have a strong and loving spiritual relationship. My feeling of connectedness with my daughter is extremely strong. She is very much a part of my life and always will be. I have redefined my relationship with her and do the things I want and need to do in order to keep our love and connection alive.

When I found out this talk was scheduled for the Fourth of July, Independence Day, I decided that the theme of my talk would revolve around independence. As a grieving parent or grandparent what kind of independence do we want? It's as if we need to establish our own *Bill of Rights* as bereaved parents. Now, your Bill of Rights will most likely be different from mine, but maybe there will be some things we share that can help us all.

Some of our desired freedoms may be unrealistic, such as,

- Freedom from this constant pain.

- Freedom from those rushes of panic when we realize for the millionth time what has happened.

- Freedom from the yearning ache to hold and kiss our child.

But there are some freedoms we can and should expect. I am going to talk about two of them, though I know there are many more.

Freedom From Lack of Understanding

As I mentioned, I have tried to educate others, particularly psychologists, about what we go through as bereaved parents. This includes a lot of different people though, like ministers, co-workers, therapists, your family, friends, and multiple others in your life. Which means I need to share my story with them and try to give them insight about some of the things they need to know. Let me share a little about some of the things I have told them.

- Appreciate the value of a hug, a simple holding of the hand, a touch on the arm, and a soft whisper that you are sorry.

- Remember that saying the child's name aloud and perhaps a remembrance of them is the greatest gift you can give to a bereaved parent.

- One of the things you hear a lot is: "I just can't imagine what you are going through." My learned response to this is, I don't want you to imagine, I want you to remember Maria-Victoria's smile and laughter.

- Listen! Listen! Let the bereaved parent talk. Never judge or try to fix what you interpret in your mind as the wrong thing to do. If it brings comfort to the bereaved, it is just fine. Remember, judgmental utterings HURT!

- Learn to say something like, "That sounds so interesting." "I am so glad it has brought you comfort."

- Remember that people grieve and rebuild differently. In our *Compassionate Friends* meetings, we have learned firsthand the notable differences between males and females in how they process hurt and the future without their child.

Freedom to Build My Life, My Way...

...to redefine my relationship with my son or daughter and to do and believe in what works for me. Boy is that a mouthful. Another way to put it, we have a right to seek hope and comfort.

This is a BIG one! It is probably the most important freedom on the bereaved parent's Bill of Rights.

When we suffer a loss of someone we love, it is hard to come to terms with what this profound change means for our lives. We know in our hearts that the love we feel can't just stop. This is as incomprehensible to us as the reality of death itself. I believe that this is the first lesson I learned on my journey. Love is not a physical thing; it is a purely spiritual presence. Although physically, my daughter, or your son or daughter or grandchild, is not here with us, the spirit, the essence of our children *is always* with us.

It is a strange and disconcerting feeling to feel intense love and intense grief at the same time. We, as Compassionate Friends, know better than most how intensely *personal* grief is. Even though we may have our compassionate friends, our regular friends, our spouses, our family, it is still personal. Surely no one could feel the enormity of grief I feel, I believe and say to myself. I believe no one could possibly understand this wrenching pain. But then I look at the faces looking up to me now and realize we are all one.

My own spiritual growth has been profound since embarking on this excursion into spirit over seven years ago. I have replaced the Why? The Why me? The What if? Questions of fresh, raw grief with different questions that I will embrace as I travel up the spiritual highway. After this passing of time, my questions are now different.

- How do I give my love to you now, honey?
- How do I keep our spiritual connection strong?
- How have I grown as the result of this experience?

This last question is of immense importance because the answer to it is the reason to continue to live. I don't pretend to know the answer, but I will continue to search for it. Have I grown as the result of this experience? Yes, and I continue to grow.

There is a Chinese proverb which says, "The man who moved mountains began by carrying away small stones."

So, it is with the mountain of grief.

Our spiritual journeys will all be different. We will be influenced by the various directions we take, the travelers we encounter, the ideas we embrace. There is no one map to follow, no travel agency that will guarantee a safe and hazard-free journey. There is no right way, there is only what works for you. I would like to share some of my own landmarks on this personal journey in the hope that some common occurrences among us will assure us that we are never alone.

It has been seven years since Maria-Victoria died. In some ways these years have been incredibly fast; in some ways excruciatingly long. Our lives have been defined by the death of our child. We are no longer the same people we once were. We have changed dramatically. The pain we feel cannot be described to others. It is ever-present, sometimes overwhelming; sometimes like being in quicksand where you are fighting not to drown in your own sorrow. It takes tremendous courage to live with this constant pain.

I remember shortly after Maria-Victoria died, of having a rather exquisite feeling of peace and a sense of being *blessed* to have this experience. Now it is strange to feel blessed when you have lost the one you love so much. This is not something I would have shared with other people, and I certainly couldn't understand it at the time. This feeling of blessing conveyed that I was going to learn what love was all about and see it at a depth others can't, unless they have experienced what we have.

When I look back, I know I was being prepared for this particular journey in my life; my daughter was too. In the first year of my new life, I did a lot of writing, much of it, I believe, inspired by a continuing communication with Maria-Victoria.

One paragraph in particular captures the essence of our time together here.

> We were *together* before either of us was born on this
> Earth. We were the closest of friends, soul mates,
> who loved one another and had a very special bond.
> We chose to be born in the circumstances we needed.
> You chose me to be your mother. I chose you to be my
> daughter. We had different purposes for being here on
> Earth. Your spiritual growth was almost complete, you
> didn't need a lot of time here. Although I'm not sure
> what your growth and mission was, I believe it involved
> the true understanding of unconditional love, the free
> giving of love, and learning to value yourself. You were
> also here to help with the growth of many, many other
> souls, including mine. You have completed your mission
> and growth and are now waiting for me to finish mine.

One of my favorite sayings, which has become much more powerful after Maria-Victoria's death: *Coincidence is God's way of staying anonymous.*

Oh, how I believe this!

So many things that have happened to me during the past seven years have confirmed that my daughter and I are still very much together and very much in love. I have flown with my daughter in dreams; I have had countless experiences of exquisite *coincidence* that have reaffirmed our love.

From these many experiences, I want to share with you eight little stories about the permanence of love when you open your heart and eyes to what you can see. I've given these stories names, and later, I invite you to look at some mementos of these experiences.

The Place

The Gift of the Red Bird

A Visit of Love

The Butterfly

Hugs from Heaven

My Angel Plays with My Angel

The Shining Light

Angel on the Road

The Place

When Maria-Victoria was five years old, she, her dad, and brother went out and stopped at a frozen yogurt store. I had been at the mall shopping by myself. On the way home, I had a *strong feeling* that I should stop and get a yogurt. Now this is not something I would normally do when I'm by myself, not at all. When I got there, I was happily surprised to see them. My kids and my husband were just finishing their yogurt, and Al was ready to leave. The kids said they wanted to stay and keep me company.

About ten minutes later, we headed out and encountered an accident at the intersection of Tara Boulevard and Mundy's Mill Road. It was Al. The car had been completely smashed like an accordion; there was no longer a back seat. Had the children been with him, Maria-Victoria would have been in the back seat and would surely have been killed. But *coincidence* had kept the children from being in the car.

Eight years later, Maria-Victoria was killed by a speeding driver at the exact same spot, *the exact same spot*, the intersection of Mundy's Mill Road and Tara Boulevard.

I was given eight more years of the most exquisite love imaginable, and for this I feel blessed.

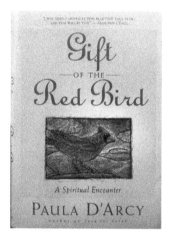

The Gift of the Red Bird

Shortly before Maria-Victoria died, we attended a funeral together for a classmate of hers. The church was remarkably beautiful with an outdoor waterfall seen through the sanctuary window. The priest, Father John, connected so well with the many children there. He reminded me of a good friend who had recently lost his son.

When Maria-Victoria died, I knew immediately that I wanted and needed to have her funeral there. I felt drawn to this church even though it wasn't mine. I also was not at all familiar with Catholic procedures. One day I decided to go to a service. I sat at the end of a pew, but knew I needed help both to make it through and to know what to do. So, I scooted over and introduced myself to the woman closest to me. Her name was Margo, and as I told her my story, she offered me comfort and love. The next Sunday, I looked for Margo, and she had a present for me. It was a book, *The Gift of the Red Bird* by Paula D'Arcy. It is an inspiring book about *the power of spiritual connection.*

Since that time, I have had countless experiences with cardinals who have let me know that my daughter is around. I have told my daughter how much I love her, and a *red bird* will come up to the window. The red bird has become a powerful sign of our continuing love and connection.

A Visit of Love

About two months after Maria-Victoria died, I was curled up in a chair in front of the fireplace. The only other person in the house was my son, who was asleep in the next room. I was in that wonderful period just before you go to sleep, and you feel totally relaxed. My eyes were closed, and I felt a presence over me, looking down on me. You know how you can feel when someone is there. The presence radiated love; I could feel it so intensely. It was a wonderful feeling. I didn't open my eyes because I didn't want it to stop.

I thought my son had gotten up, and it was him. But when I finally did open my eyes, no one was there. I checked on my son who was still asleep and had not been up at that time. To this day I still vividly remember the feeling, it was pure love. I believe it was Maria-Victoria or God—or both.

The Butterfly

Another picture in the group David's friend Andy sent was one of Maria-Victoria's outstretched arm and hand holding a butterfly. Just by itself, that would have been a momentous treasure for me. A few days later, on my way to the cemetery, I thought about the picture and said to myself, "Wouldn't it be something if a butterfly came to let me know that Maria-Victoria was around."

I laid out a blanket by her grave, got some materials to write with, and placed a picture of Maria-Victoria on the blanket for inspiration. I was engrossed in writing, and when I looked up, there was one beautiful butterfly hovering. It then landed right on Maria-Victoria's photograph and stayed there for a full five minutes. I watched it in awe, tears streaming down my face, and again I knew the power of the continuing love my daughter and I have for one another.

Hugs from Heaven

Several months after Maria-Victoria's passing, I found a roll of film I had forgotten to develop. On that roll were wonderful pictures of Maria-Victoria—but one in particular became a treasure and special gift to me. It was a picture of Maria-Victoria in a

white sweater hugging me. Mean-
while, at my former husband's house,
he also found a roll of film. When it
was developed, there was a picture
of Maria-Victoria, in the same white
sweater, hugging him in exactly the
same pose. Now these pictures were
taken at different times and in totally
different family situations.

Ten months after the accident, a
close friend of my son David sent
us some pictures he had taken on a
trip to the mountains the summer
before she died. In the pictures was
one of Maria-Victoria in the same
white sweater hugging her brother
in exactly the same way.

Some may call this *coincidence*,
but I know in my heart this is not

so. Maria-Victoria's hugs from heaven were an affirmation of
the strength of love. And, yes, I still have that white sweater!

My Angel Plays with My Angel

I must tell you about my dog, Angel. She's a Bassett hound
and as lovable as they get. Angel was born on Maria-Victoria's
birthday, April 30. She was born precisely at the time we were
dedicating a memorial garden at her school on her first birthday
after she died. It was a birthday party at her school for all her
friends, but I was the one who received the present. I have always

considered Angel to be my gift from God and Maria-Victoria. Angel receives the physical hugs and kisses I can no longer give my daughter, and she loves me right back.

I'm sure many of you are familiar with John Edward, the medium who has the TV show, *Crossing Over*. There may be some who are uncomfortable with such topics, and if so, I apologize. *Not really—remember I have the freedom to do what I need to find comfort and feel the love of my daughter.* However, I want to share with you tonight from my heart, and what I know to be true.

I had the privilege of a private reading with John Edward, shortly before he became so well known. This was by phone. He was in New York, I'm in Atlanta. There is not time to go into the details of this incredible experience. Suffice it to say that those familiar with his work think it was the most powerful reading he has ever done.

My Angel Plays with My Angel

My Angel

I do want to share a piece of it with you that even had John dazzled. I was in my office, sitting at my desk during the reading. At one point, Angel came up to my left side and started barking out of the blue. John could hear the barking through the phone and asked if that was my dog. After a slight hesitation, he said, "Your dog is going to move from your left side to your right side." Five seconds later, she did just that. He then told me that my daughter plays with Angel and, in fact, Angel is going to find a chew toy or something and play with her. Within a minute, Angel went into the next room, my waiting room, and found a little dog biscuit thing she must have hidden before. I had no idea it was there. She came back to my office, right in front of my desk, and began to jump around and throw the biscuit up into the air with her nose, over and over again. It was such an incredible sight, just beautiful spontaneous play. My heart was beating so hard, and I felt *joy*, a joy that I thought I would never feel again. John was as excited as I was. He said, "I'm in New York. It's your daughter who is there with you."

The Shining Light

We all know how difficult anniversaries are for those who have lost their children. This past September 13 was a bad one for me. We had collectively mourned September 11 and then September 13, only added to my personal grief. I made it through the day and went on to bed. At about 5:00 am, I was awakened by Angel with her typical, "I want to go out scenario." What I usually do is open the door to the basement, where she can go down and into the back yard through a special door. I didn't turn any lights on since there was a nightlight in the kitchen. Normally, this would have been routine, and I probably wouldn't have even looked down the stairs. But for some reason, this time I did look.

In the dark at the bottom of the stairs, I could see a small rectangle, and it was glowing a luminous green and white. I kept looking at it trying to figure out what it was, and I shifted around to make sure there was no light coming from somewhere that could be reflecting off whatever it was. There wasn't. Finally, I decided I had to go see what it was. I turned on the light and went down the stairs. Laying on the floor was a rectangular plaque with four hearts on it. This is what had been glowing. As I was going down the stairs, I had a thought or voice come into my head that said, "I'm behind this, Mom."

I lifted the plaque and behind it was a small picture of Maria-Victoria. I just sat down on the steps and sobbed, but it was a healing sob.

However, the scientist in me looked for an explanation. I took the plaque into a dark room to see if it glowed, it didn't. The plaque and various pictures had been on a chair in my office because I was rearranging some things and hadn't gotten around to them. My little granddaughter had been there the week before, and *maybe* she had arranged the plaque and picture and I hadn't noticed it. But what kind of explanation didn't matter. The *coincidence* of all these things happening are miracles in themselves.

Angel on the Road

In late September of this year 2003, my husband and I took a trip to Ocean City, Maryland, to visit my father. My husband wanted to take a day and go to New Jersey to visit some boyhood friends. I wasn't looking forward to this marathon driving trip and visit, but I reluctantly said I'd go to keep him company. On the way, I talked to Maria-Victoria. "Honey, give me a sign that you are around."

When we arrived at Tom's friend's house, we sat around the kitchen table and somehow the topic of my reading with John Edward came up. This had a profound effect on the family there as they were dealing with the recent loss of a loved one. I felt secure in the knowledge that there was a reason I had to come on this trip and felt that I had helped them. Our friend then told us about the lady next door who had been taking pictures and had one exposure left and nothing to take a picture of. So, she just aimed the camera up to the sky and snapped.

It was taking a long time to get her photos back, and when she inquired, she was told that Kodak wanted to buy one of her pictures.

The picture of the sky had revealed an angel. She gave me a copy of the picture. I noticed immediately that the color was

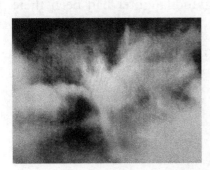

a luminous green and white, not the blue and white I was expecting. It was the same luminous green and white I had seen on the shining plaque at the bottom of the stairs. When you look at the picture, the angel is clearly visible, and when you turn it over, you see the face of a child. Was this *coincidence* or is it the sign I had requested from my daughter?

Thank you for letting me share these stories with you. Every day I feel my daughter with me. I have learned to PAY ATTENTION. I have learned that, yes, *coincidence is God's way of staying anonymous.*

Yes, bereaved parents need independence to feel, to search, to find what brings them comfort and HOPE and BELIEF. Never try to take that away from them. They are on the spiritual journey of a lifetime.

Just as all of you, I have also learned a lot about love. I have a new definition of grief. Grief is *living the love.* Please take a minute and think about the love you have for your child. Feel it, feel the enormity of that love. Grief can only happen when you allow yourself to feel the enormity of that love. We in *Compassionate Friends* are experiencing a depth of love that others don't know. We grieve by *living that love* every day.

We have learned the most profound truth of all, through the deepest pain that anyone could ever imagine, that love is eternal, and love is all there is.

I would like to close this chapter with some of my favorite quotes and sayings.

Sometimes all a person needs are a hand to hold and a heart to understand.

Love, not time, heals all wounds.

Einstein: Particles of energy that are once joined together can never really be separated.

Everyone wants to live at the top of the mountain, but all the happiness and growth occurs while you're climbing it.

Coincidence is God's Way of Staying Anonymous.

Talk to National Compassionate Friends Conference, July 4th, 2003, in Love and Honor of Maria-Victoria Boucugnani

BACK FROM THE FUTURE

This was the time when I really began to consolidate my beliefs. Actually, coming to terms with your own beliefs and being able to put them in words is a crucial part of this spiritual journey. It is far more than what you may have been taught in your particular religion or by your parents. I believe it requires experiences that you *know* are real to mold and shape your beliefs with richness and truth as well as faith. Then, and only then, do you know exactly what you believe.

I had also made my "choice" by this time. I had a new perspective on my relationship with my daughter. It was, and still is, vibrant, constant, and an everyday occurrence. Our emphasis is on memories of happiness, frequent talks, pictures, mementos, and sayings all over the house that make me feel totally connected.

Now, I must emphasize once again, that this is what I needed and wanted. Not everyone will be the same. I have a friend, a professor, who lost his nineteen-year-old son in a drowning accident on a river. When we talked, he told me he simply couldn't stand to have pictures of his son or objects around, as the memory of his death was simply too hard for him to take. We differed so much in this way, but I respected his decision and what he needed. We all must do that, we simply must.

The necessity of promoting a "freedom from lack of understanding" in the bereaved parents' Bill of Rights should be a part of the education of all those in the helping professions but are good for all of us to know and abide by. Most importantly, professionals, friends, and family need to both respect and value the individual's need to chart their own course and form their own beliefs. Remember, no one really knows exactly what happens to us after we die. Not a single soul can tell you the answer to that question. No one should dictate to you what you *should* or *must* believe. It just doesn't work that way. Your heart should resonate with your beliefs. It is only through this route that peace can be found.

The experiences I have had to confirm my beliefs are profound and extraordinary. I wish that all could experience this. "The Place" reaffirms my belief that I was given eight more years of love from my daughter and eight more years that I could give her love. What a gift! Seeing that extra time as the greatest gift that could be given by God reframed her death in a totally different perspective. No, it did not take away the pain and despair, but it blessed me with the belief that our spiritual journeys are the most important and meaningful parts of our lives.

The *Gift of the Red Bird* reaffirmed the value of turning to compassionate others when your spiritual heart needs replenishing. It also added to what I was continuing to learn about the connectedness of the universe and our ability to communicate across dimensions through love.

I will never, ever forget the feeling I had during "A Visit of Love." This intense, radiating feeling of love is almost indescribable. I *know* it was a gift from God.

In retrospect, the message was definitely about the

permanence of love, a comforting blanket to take care of me, to assure me that everything was all right, that love is so strong, so perfect that it will never go away.

I still have the chairs this occurred in, recovered now from green to yellow. They will be with me as long as I live on this earth. They are dedicated to being used for the deep talks I have with my son whenever we are together here at my home.

Remember, my favorite quote of all time from Einstein is, "Coincidence Is God's Way of Staying Anonymous." "Hugs from Heaven" is a perfect example of why I believe that. What are the chances that three almost identical pictures are found on undeveloped film from three different people in three different households taken at three different times. Each picture shows Maria-Victoria hugging the people closest to her while she is wearing the same comfy white sweater. Each comes as a hug from heaven at different times, months after she died.

David's friend Andy's picture of Maria-Victoria's hand holding a little butterfly on the trip to Helen, Georgia, was the impetus for my casual thought, or wish or prayer, that it would be wonderful if a butterfly came to visit while I was visiting and writing at her gravesite. It was no coincidence that a gorgeous butterfly hovered and then landed on her picture on the blanket and stayed there for five minutes.

Rather, it is just as plausible that it is God's way of validating (His) hand in sending peace and love. Such messages are real as long as our eyes are open, and we pay attention. Butterflies are often a symbol of communication to those who have lost loved ones. But this was truly, truly amazing and awe-inspiring. When you recognize these messages, they have the power to soothe and heal and help to mold your own belief system. They bring joy that will make you cry, but joy sometimes does that.

"My Angel Speaks to My Angel" was at the culmination of a truly extraordinary reading by the medium John Edward. Those who are familiar with his extraordinary strength in this area, feel it is likely the most powerful reading he has ever done. Almost the entire reading was spot on, extremely accurate with revelations there was simply no way he could have possibly acquired any information about beforehand. As a scientist, and also because I wanted truth and to protect myself, I was vigilant about not providing any information that could be identifiable before the reading. I did not give my last name when making the appointment, I sent a money order instead of a check for the fee, and took every precaution I could think of. I was also very careful in how I responded to what he said to me, never volunteering new information, only acknowledging the veracity of what he was saying. John does not want people to record his readings, and I honored that, but I am extremely fast and accurate in writing notes and notably attentive.

My mom was the first to immediately come through. She gave him the number twenty-eight which is my birthday and also my son's birthday. He reported that she had breast cancer that went to her head. He also spontaneously noted that it was detected early, was better, then came back. All accurate. He reported specifics such as her *throwing in the towel,* though he was somewhat hesitant in saying that. (I had been with her but went back home forty-five miles away.) Right when I stepped inside my house, I got the phone call that she had passed away and had to come back immediately.

His phrasing was, "You had to travel to her when she died. It's like you were there and left and then had to go right back."

John then spontaneously said, "You have a brother." My response was simply, "Yes."

He told me my mom was giving him the feeling that he is distant, not connected as much. Any person who knows my brother will recognize that immediately.

The next to come through was my grandmother. John's exact words were, "There's an older woman here that's not your mother but was like a mother to you. She helped raise you. It's your grandmother. She has a sister with her."

(Notice how things just come spontaneously—there is no searching—just immediate factual information.)

The sister is my Great Aunt Polly. John then said that either my mom or grandmother was telling about a ring I had. He also said that he doesn't usually like to do jewelry, because nearly everyone has jewelry from a loved one, but he went on to describe it. "Looks like silver leaf on gold with tiny diamonds, one in the middle and two to the side."

My response was "Yes! I'm looking at it right now. I wear it all the time."

John's response, "No kidding!"

John then gave something very specific that at first I didn't register. He stated, "I'm getting something from your mom's side. It reminds me of *Gone with the Wind* and Tara. Something like a passed down story from the Civil War in your family. It's not a war story but involves *the plight of a heroine*. It's coming from your grandmother."

I then stated, "I don't know."

John said, "Well, if there's someone you can ask, see if it rings any bells."

I think because I focused on the *story* part, the most obvious thing didn't immediately register. My daughter was killed on *Tara* Boulevard, the plight of a *heroine in the family*.

John was also accurate in stating that there were *parallels* between all of us. My Mom, Grandmother, and Me. He was given his sign for parallel; my grandmother lost her daughter and I lost mine, both were our youngest children. Also, I was born on Thanksgiving and my grandmother died on Thanksgiving night when I had gone up to visit her in Maryland with my baby David, so she could see him for the first time.

John then correctly identified where I was living now as my *second place* and encouraged me to finish the *garden*, I had wanted to put there in honor of someone.

Then spontaneously, John stated, "Who passed with head problems? This is a very dominant energy, usually this is male but doesn't have to be."

My response, "My daughter."

John, "And who has the D sound in his name?"

My response, "My son, David."

John then stated, "Your daughter is telling me she passed from a blow external to her head. She was in the wrong place at the wrong time. She says it hit the side and back of her head, the right side and behind. It takes her right way."

(As a neuropsychologist, I made myself read the autopsy report. The blow had been to the right side of her brain— parietal and temporal and a little occipital (back) region. Maria-Victoria had been turned left looking at her brother and talking to him when the van hit the passenger side.)

John's next utterance, "The person who did this was out of control, there was a lack of control, like he was inattentive."

Then immediately John said, "Did he run a red light or something?"

My response, "Yes."

(The investigation revealed that the driver of the van that hit their car was speeding and had run a red light. The driver said he was distracted by a puppy that was in the van.)

John then added, "He hit the passenger side, and I am getting north."

(They were heading north before the left turn off Tara Boulevard.)

I think you can imagine how blown away, excited, and in awe I was by this time. I was alone in my office where it is extremely peaceful and quiet.

John then spontaneously added, "Why am I getting

this weekend feeling? Like the weekend was coming, and she was getting ready for the weekend. Did this happen on a Friday night?"

My response, "Yes!"

(The accident was Friday, September 13. Maria-Victoria was planning to go out to the movies with some girlfriends that night.)

John then simply stated, "There were two people in the car. The other person is older than she is. It's a male. It's her brother. He is five years older than she is. He needs to know she's okay."

(Notice how matter of fact, spontaneous, and quick this was said to me.)

John also said that my daughter was showing him the movie, *Ordinary People.* "That's my sign for knowing that David has been carrying around a tremendous amount of survivor's guilt. She wants him to know it was not their fault. They couldn't see what was coming."

John also correctly noted that David was briefly unconscious, and not with it after the accident.

(In a later discussion with my son, he acknowledged that he had suffered from much survivor's guilt and had been plagued with nightmares, especially the first six months to a year after the accident.)

John also stated that Maria-Victoria wanted David to know that she had visited him, but his nightmares were not her, just his brain trying to deal with it.

John then said, "Who is Kristin?" followed shortly by, "Who is Heather?"

My response was, "Friends of my daughter."

John said, "She wants to let them know that she is okay."

Both names were said with no hesitation. You may remember Kristin as the one who left the beautiful card, note, and angel that was described at the end of "A Grief Shared."

John then asked me, "What is that big table-like thing you are sitting at?"

(Remember John is in New York, we are doing this by phone.)

My response, "I'm sitting in my house at my big desk in my office."

John said, "She is telling me that directly to your left is something that you have put there as a remembrance of her."

My response, "I don't believe this! The only thing to my left is a beautiful portrait of an angel that I specifically bought from an artist. I had it framed and placed there to remind me of my daughter when I'm in my office."

The artist's drawing of an angel I had put directly to the left of my desk as a remembrance of my daughter.

John added, "She also says there's *baby pictures* around the desk. Not necessarily pictures of a baby, but baby pictures."

My response, "I have two miniature pictures of my daughter and David on the credenza behind my desk."

(John's way of phrasing this was remarkable. What better way to describe miniature pictures.)

These baby pictures will stay with me forever. They are still here after 27 years.

These are the "baby pictures" that were on the credenza behind my desk—miniature pictures

John said, "Gosh! The anniversary of her passing, just passed."

My response, "Yes, it was September 13". *(This was September 28.)*

John said, "Who's Mar– Marra?"

My response, "Maria. That's my daughter. Her name is Maria-Victoria."

John said, "Whew! I would have never gotten the Victoria. I can almost always get the first letter or overall sound."

John said, "She says the memorial for her was awesome. She is very thankful for it and for all the basic energy that came from it."

The funeral/memorial *was* awesome. It was full of music, especially from the *Secret Garden* and so packed with young people of her age. The main speakers were her very beloved teachers, and it was meant to be uplifting and a celebration of the girl she was; the epitome of one who cares about others, the world, the immense value of kindness and compassion, and one whose spiritual development was likely complete. My good friends sang, played music, and joined Father John in ministry.

It was at this point that my dog, Angel, entered the picture as I have described in "My Angel Plays with My Angel."

This reading was the most important and meaningful port of call on my spiritual journey through all these years. It is difficult to describe the feelings I had that day. Without an ounce of doubt, I *knew* that my daughter was all right, that our love was strong and unbreakable. I knew that God is Love and Love is all there is and that *it is so wonderful to realize and feel that*. I knew in an instant the power of love. That death is just a simple transition, and that if we have loved, it is forever. *It is something I now just know.*

I spent about twenty minutes talking to John Edward after the reading was completed. John is like the guy next door. He told me about having doubts about whether he should go on with this work, sharing that he sometimes wonders if he can deal with all the demands. This was September 1998, and he was about to embark on major changes such as the beginning of his TV show, *Crossing Over*, books he would write, and he was very quickly becoming well-known. I told him he just had to continue. That what he did meant so much to many people. That his work gave us *hope*, and hope is the one thing you cannot live without.

I had also done much research and reading on mediumship. I knew, of course, that there are some charlatans out there. However, I had read the work of the most validated and examined mediums, and I had an open mind and knew the difference between them.

If you are helping a friend who has such experiences or if you are in the helping professions and working with them, your job is to listen, to perhaps be amazed, to validate their experience and the comfort it has provided. You have no right to tell them they are wrong or to attempt to belittle their experiences or beliefs after their experiences.

Seeing that shining green and white light at the bottom of the darkened stairway to the basement was another unexplained phenomenon that I do not believe was a coincidence. The fact that it was emanating from a heart plaque that my beloved friend Janice gave to me was extraordinary by itself. However, hearing in my mind the actual words, "I'm behind this Mom," as I was going down the stairs and then finding a small picture of Maria-Victoria underneath the plaque is a series of *coincidences* that scientists are now examining with the possibility that they reflect a higher intelligence or God behind the workings of the universe. This is a merging of science and spirituality.

The work of Dr. Gary Schwartz at the University of Arizona is especially pivotal in this area of inquiry. He has formally and scientifically studied both the work of well-respected mediums such as John Edward and what are referred to as super synchronicities as examples of this postulate. Please refer to the recommended reading at the end of this book for some of his many publications.

The *coincidences* or synchronicities associated with "Angel on the Road" are just another example of the veracity of Einstein's famous quote. I asked Maria-Victoria to give me a sign that she was around, the family we had dinner with had just lost a loved one, they were helped and enthralled by the discussion of the reading I had with John Edward, they told me about the next-door neighbor who had taken the picture that Kodak wanted to buy, and the picture was a picture of an angel, and when you put it upside down, was a picture of a child. That is actually six different coincidences at once or a super synchronicity. Since I have had so many unusual experiences, it is easy for me to believe that this truly was the sign I asked for and provided to me in a rather remarkable way.

Coincidences? NOPE!

About one year after I had the reading with John Edward, my husband and I went on a cruise to Alaska. There was another medium onboard, James Van Praagh, who was giving seminars during the trip. There were tons of people on this elegant *Celebrity* cruise, and a small portion were probably there because of the seminars.

Anyway, we had a formal dinner every night, and we were seated at a table for four with another couple, much younger than us.

Jim and Tami were wonderful, and we were delighted that they would be our dinner partners for the rest of the week. At the first dinner, totally out of the blue, with no hint from any of us, Jim and Tami shared how they had recently attended a large group reading with a medium named John Edward.

They asked if we had ever heard of him? Without waiting for our answer, they enthusiastically began telling a story he told the audience there about a lady he did a reading for and how at the end, he had told the lady that her daughter was telling him that she played with her dog and that the dog would get a dog biscuit or something from somewhere and play with her. Imagine our shock, and their shock, when we told them that was ME!

They said that John told the audience he was blown away by what had happened, and obviously, it affected them since they relayed the story innocently to us. It was remarkable! It was affirming!

Yes. It was God's way of staying anonymous.

Here is a TEST
to find whether *your*
mission on earth is
finished: If you are *alive*,
IT ISN'T.

– RICHARD BACH

CHAPTER FIVE

Physicians, Physicians –
Do No Harm and Continue
to Do Good Work

I wrote in "A Grief Shared" about the physician telling me in a very cold and dispassionate manner that my daughter was *deceased*.

The way I was treated by that doctor in the emergency room really grated on me. Many of us who have lost children perhaps find some relief (or purpose) in embracing a *cause* that we feel can help the world and give a legacy to our child. These are often very powerful and can lead to lasting changes in our society for the good of all.

One of several that come to mind is the work of friends Rae Ann and Steve Gruver. They lost their eighteen year old son, Max, in a fraternity hazing at LSU. This practice has resulted in the death of so many young, promising people. The Gruvers have travelled the country speaking to college students in an effort to stop this insane tradition.

They have been successful in changing laws and bringing those responsible to accountability. This has also been the case in other deaths, where parents were instrumental in changing laws.

In my case, I really couldn't find one. Yes, the *perpetrator* was speeding and ran a red light. He was inattentive; not by a cellphone—but by a puppy.

It just didn't feel right. In fact, two days after the accident, I tried to contact this man through the owner of the business he worked for. I felt a strong need to forgive him.

Numerous newspaper articles were published about the accident. They wrote about Maria-Victoria's life, and about her school and how students were remembering her.

If I were in his position, I would think such forgiveness would help me. However, his boss told me that they had been advised by their attorneys not to have any contact due to legal implications. A healing opportunity lost.

There was, however, something that did feel right.

I was contacted by CNN to do a story about my experience at the hospital and with the emergency room doctor. I don't remember how they knew about it. My guess is that since "A Grief Shared" had been widely disseminated at that time, they could have heard about it there.

As it turned out, Emory University School of Medicine was considering a new program to *train* doctors how to show empathy, and comfort, when they had to deliver bad news to parents and families.

CNN wanted to come to my home and do a video story about Maria-Victoria and my ER experience. Since I am a neuropsychologist, I could explain why this is so important. It would be used to train physicians. Well, this I could do!

They spent several hours with us. They videoed our home both inside and outside, while my husband and I talked about the experience, and at the same time, we were able to share the wonderfulness of my daughter.

It was helpful to me because I could let it go afterward. I received notes after it was broadcast, and I hope that it made a difference in improving the skills of physicians in training.

There are several physicians who have been instrumental in my own spiritual journey, although they are unaware of it. That has been another learning experience; most of the time we never know what our impact has been on others we have encountered in our lives. We are probably less aware of the good we have done if we are naturally kind, caring, and compassionate, like my daughter was.

The first of these physicians is **Dr. Raymond Moody** who wrote *Life After Life*. He coined the phrase NDE's, and his book began my life-long interest in Near-Death Experiences. The similarities reported among the myriad of individuals who had experienced them fascinated me.

Soon after his book was published, there was an explosion of studies and reports of NDE's, often by physicians. Many had patients, including children, who gave reports of what had occurred when they clinically died; what they saw, what they heard, even what they smelled, and most interesting of all, what they felt.

The majority of people who have experienced an NDE, do not want to return to their bodies. Reluctantly, they came back, when it is explained that it is not their time, and they had unfinished things in this life.

With my science background, I was particularly drawn to books, articles, or reports by a lot of physicians, who either had NDE's or studied them. These included physicians such as Dr. Eben Alexander, a neurosurgeon; Dr. Mary Neal, an orthopedic spine surgeon; Dr. Richard Eby, D.O.; Dr. George Ritchie, a psychiatrist; Dr. Pim van Lommel, a cardiologist; and many others.

I was most interested in whether near death experiences and the science that could be applied to them, would link to established religious or spiritual practices. I believe this is a helpful line of inquiry for anyone who has suffered a great loss and has the potential to bring peace and hope to all of us who are traveling on a spiritual journey.

One of the most important characteristics of the pioneers in the revelation and study of near-death experiences, was an open mind. It is so important to not close your mind to the possible and take delight when you find links to your own beliefs.

For those who do not feel that they can do a comprehensive study of near-death experiences, there is an excellent book by **John Burke,** *Imagine Heaven: Near-Death Experiences, God's Promises, and the Exhilarating Future That Awaits You.*

This book compiles many of the studies, actual experiences, and writings from individual books. It links them to parts of the Christian Bible. It would certainly be a good read and gives a lot of information and comfort to anyone with an interest in NDE's.

I believe just about everyone is interested in what happens to us after we die. However, my own research and study on NDE's was instrumental in forming my own beliefs and *knowings*, along with the extraordinary *happenings* I have experienced.

Following are a few examples that may lead you to consider your own beliefs and help you on your spiritual journey.

First, a look at some of the commonalities seen among the reports given by people who have experienced an NDE. Most report being out of their body, that they were floating above the ceiling of their hospital room, accident site, or wherever it occurred for them. At times, they went through walls, or outside, allowing them to report things seen from a very high vantage point.

Most also reported that their senses were heightened, and that they were more aware and alert than normal, even though they had clinically died. They were often able to report exactly what they observed below them, in detail. Additionally, about seventy-five percent reported very positive emotions, feelings of peace, and love, which they found difficult to describe in human words.

A common report involved encountering a mystical, brilliant white light, which sometimes seemed to permeate everyone and everything they saw. Both mystical beings, and/or deceased family and friends, were frequently encountered.

Generally, a majority report what can be regarded as heavenly realms different from anything they had ever encountered on Earth. This was accompanied by learning and understanding advanced knowledge not in their previous repertoire.

Another common report from those experiencing a near-death event involved a difference in their concept of time and space; both were altered. More than half reported they were aware they were returning to their body, and that they decided to do this.

Somewhat less common, but still notable were reports of passing through what seemed like a tunnel or dark space, a life review, and encountering a barrier or obstacle of some kind.

Dr. Mary Neal was trapped under water for fourteen minutes while on a canoeing excursion. Wedged under rapids, she reported that she never experienced fear or panic, but seemed more alive than she ever had felt. Dr. Neal also noted that at one point after surrendering to the will of God, she felt an incredible feeling of peace and calm. She likened it to being held in someone's arms. She tried everything she could to help herself, and after being underwater fourteen minutes, her body broke free and she tumbled down the rapids. In her words, "I felt as if I had finally shaken off my outer layer, freeing my soul."

Dr. Neal then found herself in the presence of a large group of beings, both spirits and those with physical bodies. While under water, she had a life review in the embrace of a being that she identified as Jesus. Of note is her report that without any doubt, those who greeted her in physical bodies, she had known and loved as long as she had existed.

There was great joy and the purest of love in a world that was more colorful, beautiful, and intense, than anything she had ever encountered. She also saw how emotionally devastated her friends were when they saw her recovered body by the river, and she asked to return.

Dr. Richard Eby was helping a friend clean out an apartment and fell from two stories, landing on concrete. His skull completely broke apart, and a large blood vessel in his brain was severed. He was pronounced dead on impact and taken to the morgue.

While dead, he reported that he saw himself just as he had been before, only clothed in a pure white, transparent gown. He could see through his body; he had no internal organs, allowing him to see flowers and other objects not only around, but through him. He had clear, focused, and unlimited vision.

Dr. Eby further reported, "My mind which worked here with electric-like speed answered my unspoken query, they are not needed, Jesus is the Life here. He is the needed energy."

After spending ten hours lifeless in the morgue, Dr. Eby miraculously revived but maintained his awareness of the indescribable love he felt while he visited heaven.

As **John Burke** describes in his book, *Imagine Heaven:*

"We won't lose our earthly identity; it will finally be known to use fully. We won't lose our humor, our unique personality, our unique look, our emotions, or our history and memories. We will finally be ourselves, fully. We will be all this without the confusion and wounds and lies that clouded our true identity.

I feel like the reason people experiencing a NDE say, "I feel like I'd been here before" or "I feel like I had always existed," is because you did exist in the mind of God eternally! In heaven, we get clarity on who he intended us to be before we were born.

Something I have come to realize and truly believe is that we are all here for a specific purpose. As John Burke, after his exhaustive study of near-death experiences states, "God has us uniquely here for a purpose—and love is central to that purpose—whatever else we accomplish."

This is so very congruent to what I believe. God is Love and *Love is All There Is."*

Another interest of mine is the merging of science and spirituality. I now realize, better than I ever have before, the congruence between our science knowledge and what religious teachings have stated. There is so much common ground and explanation that can incorporate both viewpoints.

I believe heaven is another dimension, incredibly more intense, beautiful, constantly compassionate, full of joy, and love beyond imagination. There are parts of the Bible I still don't believe in and challenge, but now that I understand it is all about love, that takes precedent.

Some people who have experienced NDE's have commented that their earthly experiences are now cloudy, less focused, and nowhere near the vibrancy, realness, and majesty of Heaven.

This can lead one to feel that Heaven is the reality, and life as we know it here on earth, is just a dream. I have no problem with that. I also believe, and my study of NDE's has fortified my belief, that any great loves we have had here on earth will continue eternally after we leave.

I encourage all to look at the **Recommended Reading List** to further explore your understanding of NDE's and what they can teach you. I just wanted to give you a taste, to spark your interest, and affirm that having an open mind is essential to this journey. Let me end this chapter with another report in John Burke's marvelous book that really touched my soul.

Richard Sigmund, a messianic Jew, died after an extremely horrific car accident. His injuries included a broken back, neck, both arms, and two ribs puncturing his heart. Medics said he had been dead for about eight hours when they found him.

"I was walking through a garden that stretched for as far as I could see in either direction. And I saw great groups of people. On either side of the pathway was the richest turf-green grass I had ever seen. And it was moving with life and energy. There were flowers of every imaginable size and color along the path. The air was filled with their aroma, and they were all humming. I asked if I could pick one to smell, and I was told that I could. It was wonderful. When I put the flower down, it was immediately planted and growing again. Again, there's no death in heaven. The beautifully manicured park was filled with huge, striking trees. They had to be at least two thousand feet tall. And there were many varieties. Some I knew; others, I had no idea what species they were. There was a continual sound of chimes coming from the leaves (of one tree) as they brushed against one another. The fruit was pear-shaped and copper colored. When I picked it, another fruit grew in its place. When I touched the fruit to my lips, it evaporated and melted into the most delicious thing I had ever tasted."

ALL,
everything I understand,
I understand only
because I love.

– LEO TOLSTOY

CHAPTER SIX

If Grief Was a Song

15 Years in the After

Smile, though your heart is breaking...

The first few years in the *After* were survival boot camp. You don't really know if you can survive, you can't imagine it, you're not sure you want to. You make your decision, and you plow through the *After*. It's not dark, but it's very cloudy. A thick fog—obscuring the future you don't want to see anyway.

If you're lucky enough to have friends and support, you are able to travel a little steadier. In the early months of the *After*, you cannot imagine ever laughing again. You will find that after you are able to do so, you have reached a very important milepost.

When there are clouds in the sky, you'll get by...

You'll get by is a good phrase for those of us who have experienced this loss. For a long time, that is about all you are hoping to do, *get by*. I had, and still have, an overwhelming fear of literally being suffocated by my own grief and sad shock; that it will utterly take everything out of me and leave me with nothingness. Sad shock is the combination of the realization that this has really happened, followed by the overwhelming sadness that accompanies that realization. You learn these little tricks to keep this monster at bay. I will allow myself to sink into the abyss for only a very short period of time and then rapidly climb out, or I take a conscious detour, if I'm getting too close to the edge.

What has helped me the most is a very personal thing that, originally, I seldom shared with others. It is the way I keep my daughter present with me every day. (Although I know she probably has better, more important things to do.)

Maria-Victoria's presence permeates my home. There are pictures everywhere. I can talk to her; tell her I love her and have framed notes from her telling me she loves me too. At the bottom of the stairs going to my office complex, I have put an enlarged picture of Maria-Victoria's beautiful face. Very frequently, when I go downstairs, I either talk to her, do pretend nose kisses that we always used to do, or cup my hands and blow out a big breath saying aloud, "Take this love and spread it all around the world."

We refer to the guest bedroom in our house as Maria-Victoria's room, since when we moved about a year after the accident, we decorated it the way she had wanted in our old home with the sun, moon, and stars. With every trip we take, we are accompanied by Patrick, her stuffed dog, so that she always sees the sights with us. I wear an angel pin *every day* whenever I leave the house, so she is with me. I have done this for fifteen years.

Since she left us, I've had awesome, incredible spiritual experiences assuring me and my soul, that my Maria-Victoria is still my daughter; that her spirit, her consciousness survives. It is so hard to try to explain this to people. It is incredibly important to me, such a part of who I am, that I can't bear to listen to the naysayers or worse, those who outright chastise me, because I am scientist, for believing in such things.

Yes, I am a scientist, and I have devoted a lot of time and research to the scientific study of survival of consciousness. Not to mention that I've experienced wondrous things. We who have *reluctantly* joined the group of bereaved parents, *Compassionate Friends*, probably know more about this than anyone on the planet.

If you smile through your fear and sorrow...

You do learn to laugh and smile again. You are a changed person; you now live in the *After*. With all this elapsed time, how do I describe what it feels like? The one thing that stands out the most is that I have no fear of death. This has continued from the earlier *After* years. I'm not in a hurry. I still want to enjoy life, try to have fun, do meaningful work, make a difference, and treasure my family, but I'm not afraid to die. This is very freeing and has allowed me to chart my own path. As I said in my earlier article, death is the door to where my daughter is. I view it as a great adventure with the ultimate joy of reuniting with Maria-Victoria.

I am a more *take it or leave it* kind of person now. I guess those of us who have traveled this journey have a clearer vision of what's important and what is not. I don't need to convince anybody of anything. I've become more tolerant and less tolerant. More tolerant of different points of view but less tolerant of narrow-mindedness, silliness, or arrogance.

Smile and maybe tomorrow...

I do fall into the chasm of *what might have been*. Usually, it's when I'm feeling sorry for myself, missing the physical love my daughter could be giving me at this time, and the additional grandchildren that would be a part of my life. I miss the best friend I know she would have been. That hurts—so I don't stay there long. I miss most her adorable face, her big eyes looking straight into mine, the feel of her skin on my hands, her tenderness, our bond. Thinking of her and visualizing her—that helps.

If I was asked, what do you think is the biggest misconception of people who do not understand those of us who live in the *After*? I would say they cannot understand how we keep our loved one with us, so present in our lives every day, even after what seems an impossible fifteen years.

Every day you experience both the joy of having had your child with you, and at the same time, the grief of not having your child.

I truly believe that most people think we have *moved on*, or something like that. Nope, that doesn't happen. Every day in the *After* we feel for our child. Fifteen years is 5,475 days. I can't put into words what 5,475 days has done to my body and mind. It has definitely caused erosion, a deep canyon. My soul, however, is enhanced, open, and full.

You'll find that life is still worthwhile if you just smile.

Our continuing journey is to make life worthwhile, without the physical presence of our child. Defining *worthwhile* is up to the individual person. I feel that if you have something to believe in, if hope is a big part of your life, if you are able to honor your child, and find meaning in your contribution to this Earth, you have a worthwhile life. *So, smile through your tears and sorrow, dare to laugh, dare to dream, and let your child's love embrace you.*

Written on the 15th anniversary of Maria-Victoria Boucugnani's angel date – September 13, 2011, by her mother, Lynda Boucugnani-Whitehead.

BACK FROM THE FUTURE

In this reflection, *Back From the Future,* there are several major topics that have come to mind for me to address. All are important. All are of value for both the bereaved and helping professionals to know, as well as those going through their own spiritual journey.

Smile, though your heart is aching...

It has been fifteen years. No, that is not possible. It couldn't be. It was yesterday or at the most, a couple of years ago.

A few years after my daughter, Maria-Victoria died, I wrote an article entitled "A Grief Shared" in which I was trying to let professionals and others know what is helpful and what is not for those of us who have lost a child. Now at fifteen years, I thought it might be time to revisit "A Grief Shared" from the perspective of someone further down the path.

It is harder to write this than the first one. I don't know why other than perhaps the accumulation of years of grief *and missingness* have eroded my stamina. But I still want to write it. Remember, it is just one person's perspective; maybe some things will resonate with others, maybe not.

Time. Time goes by so quickly. Everything is in terms of before and after. The *Before* is the refuge where smiles can come from. Those treasured little glimpses of the way we were. When I feel them, I am truly happy. But most of life is lived in the *After*.

The Importance of Music

I don't know about you, but music has always been a lifesaver, a soother, an inspiration, a relaxation, an invigorator, and an indication of love in my life. I dabbled with playing the piano as a child, and I was a singer for a while. On my bucket list was the desire to do a professional recording, which I did, honoring my Maria-Victoria. I would call it rather mediocre, but at least, it was fun, and I did it.

Maria-Victoria loved to sing, and she was good, much better than her mom. At the same ages, we both were notable sopranos in our school choruses, and we enjoyed singing together at home. But my favorite memory is singing and doing the *locomotion* in our living room. Our special mother/daughter thing; we loved doing it. Whenever I hear that song, I am transported back to that wonderful memory and can see, hear, and feel us doing our thing.

I am the type of personality that seeks to find meaning in everything. I can't help it; it just comes naturally. So, I do advise all who are traveling a journey marked by profound loss to let music *do its thing* and provide you with comfort. Embrace it, make it yours. Allow yourself to lose yourself in the emotions, the light, and peace that music can provide.

Don't Forget the Students and Teachers

Especially when we have lost a child, we are in a state of such numbness, disbelief, and catastrophe, that we may forget that there are others out there who are confused, hurt, and devastated by our child's death. We have to concentrate on living a life we don't want to live. When you think about it, there are few nonfamily people, who really get to know your child, as well as teachers and classmates.

Maria-Victoria's teachers and classmates gave me one of the most treasured gifts of all, and I encourage others to do something similar.

To help both the students themselves, and to help me, they asked students in the eighth grade at her school to write letters to me, about Maria-Victoria. I'm sure none of them realized what an enormous and exquisite gift they were giving me. I have an inch thick notebook with all their letters, and I read every one of them again, as I was writing this chapter.

I will tell you that I cried, no *sobbed*, as I was doing this. It was hard, but it was also a time for rejoicing.

I realize just how wonderful my girl was, how many people loved, respected, and admired who she was.

As a psychologist, it was also quite evident how much these kids needed help in dealing with the awful presence of loss and the reality of death that had hit their lives. Maria-Victoria was the third loss of a classmate at her school, within two years. You can see it in their words and expressions. By having them write these letters, her teachers became therapists too, along with the scores of other roles their job entails.

I remember days after the accident being interviewed by phone for a local newspaper article about the need to help classmates at her school, and for parents and teachers to recognize how hard it is for them. That's something Maria-Victoria would be concerned about. I knew that. And these letters from her classmates are *music to my ears—a priceless gift.*

You will see for yourself as I share some of the beautiful hand-written letters from her classmates.

Maria was a good friend. She didn't like people who talk nasty. She was smart and funny. I have known her since the sixth grade. – Sara H.

She was the nicest person I've ever met. She never said nothing bad about anybody. She didn't deserve to die. I wonder why God took her. Everybody around me is sad and crying. I even caught myself crying. But she didn't deserve it. It wasn't fair. I don't think there will ever be somebody so nice and as considerate as her. This is the perfect role model for everyone. Nice and full of love. Never said anything bad about anyone. It's not fair. I and others will miss her truly.
– Blake F.

The silence overwhelms me. it is broken with loud tears. Maria was a good person and a dear friend to me. I knew her well. I wish I could be more like her. In the past year three friends' deaths. I suddenly realize why people have always stressed that life is short. In this case like many others, way too short. Thinking about it now I realize that could have been anyone of us. I tryed very hard to hold back my tears yet somehow they are stronger than I am. It doesn't seem fair? – Tiffany V.

I saw the wreck when it happened because me and my friends were walking to the gas station where the wreck was. When I saw it I thought it would be another drunk driver or someone running a red light. I knew Maria. She was very smart. If any-one had to die in the accident why did it have to be her? She was perfect. She was nice, smart, and friendly. She shouldn't have had to die then, there, and how she did. – Todd W.

I remember that Maria was wonderful. You could be spreading gossip and roomers and when you came to Maria you would get a disapproving look on her and you would know it wasn't right. I just got to know her well this year, and she was so smart. She was going to be able to hand pick her future. Best person you could know. She was a beautiful person in both mental and spiritual and physical aspects. Maria wasn't the most popular person at Lovejoy Middle, but I think she was certainly the most admired. – Rich M.

Maria was the Best friend anyone would want. We went to the movies and we were the only ones who didn't try to get in the conversation with the others and we were the ones picking on the others for fun. She could never get mad at you. She was a special friend. She could understand anything. She would make a total stranger feel a good feeling. She will always stay in my heart. She loved everyone especially her brother. Maria-Victoria especially loved Chrissy, Ashley, Amanda, Saralyn, Yahaira, Jennifer, Jessica, and Inga. We all loved her. Those people were all part of the clan and we love each other as family. – Ashley R.

I didn't know Maria that well but I know she was a nice person and I wish I could've gotten to know her. It makes me scared to know that you could be driving and then all of a sudden you're gone. – Amy H.

When I was absent and I didn't know what the rest of the class was doing, she let me borrow her book and she helped me get caught up. I can't imagine what it must've been like to be in that car with her when she died. I wonder where she is right now. I can't imagine not being alive—not feeling anything. I hope she rests in peace. – Courtney

---

Maria was a really sweet girl. She was very smart and I will miss her very much.

I still can't believe that this has happened. I guess that tonight at the thing from 6-8 will let me face up to the fact that she's not coming back. It's hard to believe that someone can be here and then be gone the next minute. I'm going to go to the funeral and show my last respects to her.

Maria always had a smile on her face and she was easy to talk to. I know that her family is going through because we went through the same thing before, but I know that it has to be twice as hard to lose your child. I will be praying for the family. – Jennifer H.

If she was here today I would have been nicer to her, listen to her, and even talk to her. I've known her since kindergarten, never got a chance to talk to her. She was a very smart girl that helped me on a couple things that I got stuck on. Now she's not here anymore but if I had that chance to talk to her I would have talked to her. – Chad R. 4th Period

Why? Why did this have to happen to her. She had so much going for her! She was bright, smart, witty, pretty, kind, friendly.

I grew up with her and she used to be so shy. Now she is always talking and smiling to someone. She changed so much from kindergarten. My friends and I are always talking about how she would've been homecoming queen when we were seniors—'cause she was so pretty! – Cathryn S.

I feel like a part of my school life is gone. Yes, I cry and moan, but I know that Maria wouldn't want us to cry and moan because she's in a better place. I think that Maria would most of all want us to help each other through this situation but most of all help her family. But it's all in God's hands and I know that you shouldn't question God but I wonder why the innocent people die? But Maria along with Ryan and Caroline will always be in my thoughts and my heart as well. Now I think this makes everyone realize how precious life really is. – Renee B.

Maria was a great person, what happened wasn't fair to her or her parents and her classmates. She had everything going for her, she was smart and especially a very nice person. When I had classes with her she helped me out in any way she could. She will be missed dearly "we just gotta hold on—every day gotta rollon". – Chris S.

Maria was very nice and very friendly. I don't think that any-one would have a bad thing to say about her. She was a friend to everyone. Why did such a wonderful person have to die? Maybe it was just her time to go. What really did happen? She will definitely be missed by everyone. Some of us don't know how we will go on without her, but I think everyone should know that Maria-Victoria is in a much better place. We really need more people like her in this world. People who can listen to our problems and will never let us down. She was probably the best person I have ever known. I really will miss her. – Dana O.

———————————

I remember her as only the best. She was a rollmodel in my life. And I'm sad to have to say it took me for her to have to die to realize this. She was kind and blessed with many gifts. I might not have known her like others, she held a place in my heart still. When I found out my mother told me the Lord needs angels! So, I guess you would be a great one. She was just about as perfect as one can get. And if you knew her you loved her, and that's how I feel. – Erica

———————————

Maria was a great overall person she was a wonderful friend to so many people and a wonderful person. She was doing great academically. I am and was not one of her best friends, but I was shocked when I found out about her. I am sorry and I will miss her, eighth grade will not be the same without her. – Jason F.

Maria was my best friend so it's hard to write. Only that I do remember how I was able to talk to her so easily. In fact, I'm kind of scared because I really don't have anyone to talk to. I could tell her everything and she wouldn't make a smart comment or even laugh. She would just try to understand to the best of her knowledge. It's amazing when I think back how many things I told her and no one else. To think she left knowing so much more about me than any other person I know. I love her. And I know it would be hard accepting the fact that it will be a while before I see her again. – Chrissy H.

Maria was a very sweet girl. She was a person who you know that would make a difference in life today. She had a lot going for her and it's very tragic the way she died. I'm glad that I got to know her and I'm glad that we got to become friends. She was a good person to know. It is especially hard for her family. If I cry almost every time I think of her and it's hard to even imagine what her family must be going through. My deepest sympathies go out to them. It is very hard for some people because of this being the third person in our age group. It makes you have many flashbacks. But everyone has to remember her in a good way. She was very shy and quiet until you started to talk to her. Then she would start talking to you a lot. She was very easy to talk to and the more that you started to get to know her, the friendlier she got. She would want everyone to have good memory of her. And that's not really hard because there really wasn't any bad memories. – Stephanie H.

Maria was the nicest girl I ever known. She was nice to every-one. Nothing ever bothered her. No matter what anyone says about her that is bad none of it is true. Man, I just don't know what to say. I knew her alright you know it's just that I'm not good at doing stuff like this. But she was a smart, talented, and quiet girl. I know this is not the best one there is but that is what I have to say. – Unsigned

---

I knew Maria very well and I also grew up with her. I have always thought of Maria as being my best friend. Whenever everyone else was mean to me in front of me, she would never go along with them. She would always be nice to me. Maria had a lot going for her. She was a great, friendly person. If you ever need to talk I'll be here. – Kristen S.

This one will make you smile.

Dear Maria, Hey girl. How's the afterlife? You couldn't have left at a worse time though. Sorry I left for so long. I couldn't find my pen, and I was getting pretty mad. This doesn't look like an average note from me, does it? That's because I may let your mom see this letter, but the next one will be just between you and me. I'm going to tell the "reader" some nice things you did for me to try to make you blush. And I need to prepare you because at your funeral we're going to say so many nice things about you, you'll start to miss yourself. You gave up going on the math team because you knew

I wanted to. You didn't go in every round at the county quiz to give others a chance. Remember the orange pencil club? Or that case we tried in seventh grade for forum and lost? Oh, gosh. This letter's starting to sound rehearsed. It's just a way of letting my feelings out. I want you to know that no matter how much talking I do, I will never fully get over you and Ryan. I can't. I won't. I need to warn you. These next few days will seem very impersonal. I've met your Mom so many times, but right now all these kids are probably in her face bragging about how well they knew you, she wouldn't remember me. I feel like I've walked in on the middle of a scary movie I'd always wondered about, but never actually wanted to see. If the priest allows people to just say stuff at your funeral, I'm going to try with all my might. Even if I cry all the way through it and make a fool of myself, at least you'll be amused. Even if I can't think of anything profound to say, I too want everyone to know how special you are. Love indefinitely and increasingly (I think those are words!). P.S. Write back in a dream or something. – Saralyn M.

From Lynda: Saralyn, if you read this book, please get in touch with me. I want to find out what you became. You were so smart and fun! Somehow stand-up comedian could be one of your many potential professions!

Angel of my Heart by Amy P.

My heart beats like a drum
outside of my body.

A single tear rolls down my cheek.

I can't speak.

My voice is gone,
yet my body floods life.

I would gladly give it 2U.

No words I can find.
could ever express just how wonderful you were.

You gave so much to everyone.

You walked into a room and there was light.

U didn't die.

U've always been alive and you always will be.

The angel watching over us all.

It was you all along.

Only now you watch from heaven.

We can't see you, but we know.

You are in my heart and in my thoughts.

Forever.

From Lynda: Thank you Amy. Your poem expresses exactly how I feel.

I chose these examples as illustrations to others about how difficult and confusing the loss of a classmate can be for students. You will see that there is a wide range of ways of expressing this but some universal themes. It is important for those in the helping professions to know what is going on in the hearts and minds of children when they lose a classmate. It is shocking and for many may be the very first time they have dealt with a person of their age dying. I remember one of her friends telling me how disconcerting it was to see her empty desk in the classroom. School psychologists, therapists, counselors, and others need to help and know what to do when an event such as this occurs. I believe, the act of writing these letters was therapeutic and quite helpful to all of them.

Reading these letters was therapeutic for me, both at the time I received them and throughout this journey at certain times. I knew in writing this book that this part as well as a few others would be the most difficult, and that I would cry a lot and sob a lot. But I also feel so grateful! It came through so beautifully through her peers' words, how admired and respected my daughter was just by being herself. It also let me know that showing compassion, kindness, helpfulness, a love of learning, and devotion to what is right and good are qualities that young people embrace and appreciate, and that is one wonderful thing.

There were so many people—adults and children who wanted to come to the visitation that we had to schedule two nights of this before her funeral. For the parents especially, it can be very hard to do. However, although it may really tire one out, especially at a time of such fresh, raw grief, it is also life-affirming, a blessing and appreciated right in the heart that all of these people knew and loved Maria-Victoria and her family. I wanted to hug everyone who came to the visitations—every single one—and I hope I did. Although I had worked extensively to try to help plan her funeral, I was fortunate to be able to depend on my adult friends to make sure it ran smoothly and beautifully. It's a good thing because I remember very little of the funeral since I was in a daze, and it all became a blur. I do remember feeling wonderful about the music and singing, what everyone had to say, Father John and my friend and colleague, Fred Lacey who served as co-minister. I do remember walking down the aisle to the front of the church carrying Maria-Victoria's stuffed dog Patrick, so he could be there too.

After I received all those wonderful letters from Maria-Victoria's classmates, I sent a handwritten letter back to them. I believe, if I remember correctly, it was read to every one of her classes. My letter:

Dear Classmates and Friends of Maria-Victoria,

I want to thank you so much for the beautiful letters you sent to me about Maria-Victoria. I have read them over many times and shared them with others. They are very special to me and I will always hold them dear.

I want you to realize that by doing such a giving thing you have honored Maria-Victoria more than you'll ever know. I know it must have been hard for some of you to write and search for what to say—but I could tell your words came from your hearts. I could feel each word you wrote—like a great big hug from so many of you at once that I couldn't help but be lifted up and very happy that she had had a chance to be your friend or just to share her smile with you.

It is very hard at your age—and at my age too, to understand why something like this happens. Let me assure you that no one has the answer and it really doesn't help us to try to figure that out.

What does help is to focus on the things that Maria-Victoria taught us while she was with us. You have helped me with that in your letters. I have decided the very best thing I can do is to live my life the way she was living hers. I hope that you also can do that—in that way she will always be a part of us.

Some of the things I think we learned from her are:
- Be kind.
- Try not to do things that would hurt other people's feelings.
- Always do your best.
- Don't be afraid to love and show your feelings.
- Value friendship

- *Have confidence in yourself.*
- *Be true to your dreams.*
- *And above all, smile, and take delight in laughing, sharing and just being together.*

With love to you all,

Lynda — Maria-Victoria's Mom

Teachers—Let Me Tell You About Teachers

I believe teachers are some of the finest people on this Earth. It is why I wanted her teachers to have center stage at her funeral/celebration of her life. I have gotten to know and work with hundreds of teachers throughout my career. Many of them I count as dear friends. I also count them as blessings in my life. I still have contact with several of Maria-Victoria's teachers, and they always lighten my heart. It is good to have this kind of contact—someone who interacted deeply with my girl, so appreciated her and her character and accomplishments. I also know how devastated they were when she died. You know, Maria-Victoria may have only had thirteen years here, but she made an enormous difference in this world.

Maria-Victoria had a favorite teacher, although she adored just about all of her teachers. Her very favorite though was **Mrs. Judy Carter** who taught her in the third grade. Mrs. Carter spoke at her funeral:

"Six years ago, a little girl walked into my third-grade classroom. She had long, naturally curly hair and wore a shy smile. Her name was Maria-Victoria Boucugnani.

The year progressed and Maria-Victoria's smile never left. Sometimes that quiet smile turned into a roar of laughter—especially when I read aloud to the class, or when she got so involved in a book she was reading.

Maria-Victoria traveled many places through her books. She loved reading and read every spare minute. She was always eager to share what she had read. Her classmates selected her to be our "Reader of the Year."

During that very same year, this little girl won my heart. She never cared about being first, she just wanted to make sure she got to the same destination as everyone else. Maria-Victoria was a true friend to everyone in our classroom. With her quiet manner, she helped so many children complete a task that seemed overwhelming.

She kept her things so organized and quietly helped her friends stay organized. Never did Maria-Victoria say anything unkind about or to anyone. I felt like I knew her mom, dad, and David personally. She shared with me wonderful things about them. How did they get such a warm, loving, kind, child who seemed so adjusted to everything? Many, many times I have thought what wonderful parents you must be.

Well, the last day of that third-grade year arrived and I vividly remember having such a strange, sad feeling. This had been such a wonderful class. Normally on the last day of school everyone is rejoicing! I suddenly realized that I would never have this class again, and I would never have Maria-Victoria again!

Maria-Victoria's fourth and fifth grade years quickly passed. Each morning I looked forward to her running by my room, giving me a quick hug, and sharing with me what she was currently reading. In the afternoons, if she had time she'd run by again and quietly say, "Mrs. Carter, I'll see you tomorrow."

The day finally came when Maria-Victoria could no longer pop by my room for that quick hug. But guess what! That sweet middle school girl never forgot me. She wrote me letters. She shared with me her unsure feelings of sixth grade and the uncertainty if she really liked it. By the time my second letter arrived, middle school and sixth grade was the place to be! I always answered her letters, wondering if I'd get another one. Sure, enough I'd hear from my friend again. Maria-Victoria and I had not begun our writing this school year, but she had really been in my thoughts this past week. I was so proud of her for accepting the challenge of Beta Club president.

Their first meeting was this past week. I admit I was a little nervous—would my quiet, shy little third grade girl be able to be "loud" and "run" a big important meeting all by herself? Of course, she would!! On Wednesday night my phone rang, and it was Mrs. Hood. She immediately blurted out, "you won't believe how wonderful "MV" did today. (Mrs. Hood had told Maria-Victoria, "you've got almost every letter of the alphabet in your name, we've got to talk fast—so she had given her the nickname "MV".) She continued, "we had too much time left over at the end of the meeting, and "MV" just took charge and kept going! This is going to be the best Beta Club year!"

I wish I had been able to tell Maria-Victoria the wonderful compliments being said about her. I wish I had written her one last letter. I wish I had saved her letters that she wrote to me. I wish I could tell her that her third grade teacher still has that special place in her heart just for her!

Everyone here will miss Maria-Victoria in different ways. At school, you'll miss her at her locker, in the halls, and in her regular seat in class. I'll miss her letters and her middle school teachers telling me how much they love her. Her mom, dad, stepdad, and David will miss her in so many ways that we could never imagine. But we all have something that she has left us. We have her love, her patience, her understanding, her "never having to be first" and her smile. Maria-Victoria would want us to wear her soft shy smile and be a friend to everyone.

There's no doubt in my mind that Maria-Victoria is in a wonderful place right now. She's still wearing that sweet smile and being a true friend. I also know that today Maria-Victoria is "first in line."

– Judy Carter, *3rd Grade Teacher*

Maria-Victoria's teacher of the gifted, Libby Torbush, also wrote a poem about her:

Her liquid brown eyes drank in every detail,

As she absorbed information

Her gaze serious as we read, discussed, or investigated.

Always on alert, always paying attention,

With a crinkle of a smile and a flash of light in those bright eyes

Came the quick response, a quiet laugh, or the knowing look.

Grasping the situation, solving a problem, or writing a story,

She appreciated the world around her.

As a doe knows her way through the pines,

She knew where and how to find answers.

Never did she demand attention, but often did she deserve it.

Her winsome porcelain beauty held a keen, kind mind,

And a maturity that is rare.

As a flower's life is fleeting, so was hers.

Framed with a lovely grace and voice, she left her mark.

We treasure our memories of Maria-Victoria.

Fred Lacey, a psychologist on my staff and a minister as well, also spoke at her funeral saying:

"Make no mistake—Maria-Victoria is alright. The tears we shed are for ourselves and each other. May God bless us as we love and support each other in a way that helps resolve the grief.

We will never understand in this life why such events happen, because we see through a thick, distorted, fractured lens which alters and restricts our vision. Therefore, we must not allow ourselves to get stuck on the <u>why</u>; rather, we must move quickly to the <u>how</u> and the <u>what</u>, because the only way we can make meaning of the event right now is in the positive changes in the way we live."

There are Different Kinds of Crying

Another thing I have realized, especially while writing this book, is that there really are different kinds of crying. It's like a continuum spanning from the deepest sobbing where you can't stop and physically feel the despair in your body to crying because of utter joy and gratitude that you have been blessed with such a remarkable child. And all along the spectrum are degrees and mergings from the ends that can encompass both of these polar opposites at the same time. Yes, this despair sobbing can wear you out, and it still happens near the end of the journey as well as at the beginning. Don't be afraid of making someone cry. More than likely, your remembrance will bring the joyful, gratitude cry, a gift to the heart.

What Maria-Victoria communicated to me: *Tears nourish the Soul.*

As a final example in this chapter of things that really make a difference, I want to share with you a letter by an adult friend and colleague. In our current day of quick technology, email, and texting, sometimes a handwritten from the heart letter, means so very much.

Dearest Lynda,

The passing of Maria-Victoria from our time and earth must be straining and paining every ounce of your being. The missing her is felt in all your heart, mind, and soul. Each moment, now so long and difficult for you, is surely filled with dear memories of Maria-Victoria—making more poignant the knowing that these are limited to these brief years with her.

I sob as I write to you and imagine your state of mind today. Truly, your caring and kind guidance affected my own life most positively. What a beautiful mentor you were for me. I know that your giving to your own children must have been immense. Maria-Victoria was blessed to have your love, just as we all are blessed—your son and husband and the thousands of people who you have touched professionally with your brilliant mind and loving energy. Lynda dear, take strength from knowing that Maria-Victoria's soul

is with God and all the kindness and love which
you bestowed on her is helping move the world
toward being more positive and truly good and
sweet and that she will always be a part of this
goodness.

I pray from my deepest feelings that God now
holds you and David and all your family very
close and soothes your hearts. I pray that day by
day a path becomes more and more clear to you
that is nurturing and comforting and allows you
to once again experience joy.

Much love,

Lenore

Sometimes you just
have to DIE A LITTLE
inside in order to be
reborn and *rise again*
as a STRONGER
and WISER
version of you.

– UNKNOWN

CHAPTER SEVEN

Never-Ending Questions

18 Years in the After

Our lives after the loss of a child are filled with questions. There is so much uncertainty; the only certainty is that there are no definitive answers. But the questions never stop, and maybe by looking closely at the questions themselves, we may be better able to understand just how we can make it in the land of grief. So, this talk will be formulated around some questions that will probably resonate with you.

What is different from the time I wrote "A Grief Shared"?

I wrote that article just five years after Maria-Victoria died. Today, September 13, is the 18 anniversary of the day she died. Earlier I mentioned that I think of her a million times a day, so forgive me if there is no room in my mind for other things. Eighteen years later I don't think about her a million times a day, but the loss of her, the loss of what we would have been is there every hour of every day. It is in every cell of my body. It *is* different now.

You can still do productive work, you can laugh and even feel happiness, but it is *contained*, held in place. Joy is elusive; it is very hard to find. I honestly cannot imagine that I have been able to live eighteen years without her. There was a time when I couldn't imagine a month without her, but eighteen years! No, it can't be, it was only yesterday.

Which leads us to another question:

Does it really get better with time?

Well, the answer is yes and no. And it depends on your definition of *better*. We do get better in some ways; we may find a path and what helps us personally if we are lucky. We will likely recover our ability to think, to perform tasks and take care of things and give love and attention to others. But I would hazard to guess that the loss of our child was the defining moment of our lives. You don't want it to be, but it is. We search for meaning, more questions, and we so profoundly wish that someone could understand how we feel and comfort us. Those are basic needs: *understand us and give us comfort.*

Compassionate Friends is one of the few places where those basic needs can be met, at least partially. That is why it is so powerful. Back when I wrote "A Grief Shared," I talked about the need to let everyone I met know about Maria-Victoria 's death. I was probably looking for comfort, saying, *please help me*, silently to people who didn't really know me. That changed.

Gradually, I stopped doing that. It made people sad. It made parents scared. It kind of became an invasion of my privacy. What I really wanted was for people to understand how wonderful she was, to talk about her, about my amazing daughter. But there are not a lot of openings to do so. The question, *how many kids do you have?* always led to awkwardness and the need to explain that one of my children died at thirteen. Still, after eighteen years, I need to work on a way to deal with that question. I usually divert by talking about how many grandchildren I have.

A huge question for those of us who are in this place today is:

Why is the loss of a child so much harder than other losses?

I actually cringe when I see ads in the newspaper for *grief groups* that lump all losses together. Divorce, separation, loss of a spouse, loss of a job, and by the way, also loss of a child.

So why is it so much harder?

I don't have the answers, only my own opinion and ideas. But this is what I think. Your child *is* you. You live in your child and your child lives in you. Not only in the physical, genetic, DNA way, but you are in a large part responsible for nurturing the new extension of yourself into this world. The love for a child is like no other love. The closest we can come to unconditional love is the love for our child. When our child dies, a part of us dies with that child. We feel we have lost our capability of giving such pure love and receiving it in return. This is not the same for any other kind of loss. Imagine you are walking around when a part of you has died. We so much need for people to understand, but how can we expect them to unless they are *one of us.*

And our final question:

How do we honor our love for our child, and still take care of ourselves?

Let's begin with another question. Each one of us, whenever we think about our child who has died, at whatever stage we are in, has a question that we ask over and over, all the time.

Take a minute and think about *what that question is for you.* If you're with a friend or family member, tell them what your question is.

If you are reading this, write it here: _____

_____

_____

_____

My current, constant question to Maria-Victoria?

WHERE ARE YOU?

Your question may help guide you to be able to help yourself.

Think of mountains and valleys. The top of the mountain reflects those times when we are feeling the most positive and hopeful in dealing with our grief. Ask yourself what you were doing, what were you involved in, what brought you that tinge of joy when you thought about your child? The valleys are the times when you felt most defeated, sometimes without hope and overcome by profound sadness. Today we are not going to pay attention to the valleys, just the mountain tops.

Each of you will have different questions, different actions, and activities, at the mountain top. But for my example, *where are you?*

I realize I felt best when I read and explored everything I could to understand and form beliefs about just where Maria-Victoria is and to build hope that this was just a temporary separation. I did whatever I could to keep my connection with my daughter strong and vibrant. I felt best when I wrote and talked about Maria-Victoria. I'm going to do more of this, and I'm going to take the time to really examine my own mountaintop and try to help myself. I hope each and every one of you will examine what helps you the most and do it, *regardless of what anyone else would think.*

Do it for yourself. Sometimes climbing up that slope is very, very hard. But honor your child and yourself by spending as much time on the mountaintop as you can.

I want to close with some words of advice from Maria-Victoria. One of the things we did together that I loved so much, was to sit down with some quiet time. Each of us would share something that makes us happy, and then we would write those things in a little book. We would alternate, I would say one thing, she would say the next thing and so on. It was so good.

Here are a few of the many things that she said made her happy. *I encourage everyone to do this.* Perhaps, her words may help you too.

Soft, cool comforting sheets
Sunshine coming through the window.
That my mother took care of me when I was sick
Sausage
Listening to a puppy bark.
Vegging out when I'm tired.
Being around enthusiastic people.
That Mommy got to have a good time at Disney World.
Eating Kung Pao shrimp.
Watching Mommy being happy.
Hearing the laughter of David, Mommy, and me all together.
White colored things.
Air conditioning blowing on my face.
Finishing a really good book.
The huge bear in Mommy's office (which is mine).
The little puppy bank on Mommy's desk that stares at me.
Watching Mommy being happy.
Being organized at school.
To see Mommy's diploma on the wall.
Polar bears.
My big bed.
Sitting outside in the morning reading with Mommy.
People saying, "Are you okay?"
That we started this book.
A clean kitchen in the morning.
Seeing that my brother looks so funny when he sleeps.
Coming home on Friday and not having to do anything.

Going to the Waffle House with Amy.
Spending quality time with Mommy.
You see it's the little things that make us happy.

Talk Given September 13, 2014, Mid-Georgia Compassionate Friends 1st Annual Walk to Remember, Griffin, Georgia in Honor of Maria-Victoria Boucugnani, by Lynda Boucugnani-Whitehead

BACK FROM THE FUTURE

There are so many questions along the road of this spiritual journey. It is as if you are constantly seeing signposts along the road. They do change in quality and even in quantity as you continue to travel this rocky, winding road. It's full of pot-holes, no outlets, dead-ends, detours, and stop signs. You long for specifics. Imagine, just twenty miles until pain ends, three-hundred miles until laughter, or the exact location of the City of Serenity.

Of course, most of the early questions are short and direct. Why? What If? How do I live?

Gradually, they become more meaningful and profound and perhaps somewhat more amenable to answers. How you get those answers and whether they actually help you largely depends on the person you are.

In many ways, life on this journey and one's spiritual evolution is reflected in the kinds of questions you ask yourself over time. Although there are definitely some universal questions, the flavor of your personal questions, as well as the answers you receive, is likely a reflection of your personal place on this spiritual journey.

Think about these questions and decide if they are the kind of questions that could potentially help you or harm you.

- *What did I do that was so bad to deserve this happening to me?*

- *Why is God so angry with me?*

- *What is something good I can do to honor my child?*

- *What lessons have I learned from my child?*

- *How do I live now?*

- *How can I trust anything ever again?*

- *Where is God?*

- *What do I have to live for?*

- *How do I make my life meaningful again?*

- *Where are you?*

- *What if I hadn't been working, would this have still happened?*

- *Where can I go to get help?*

- *Can anyone ever understand what I am going through?*

- *Why bother being such a good person when you just get struck down?*

- *What is the purpose of life anyway?*

- *Why do such bad things happen to good people?*

- *I feel so angry at God. What am I going to do about that?*

- *I want to hurt the person who did this. Make them pay. Should I do that? How?*

- *What would my child want me to do? What would he/she say to me?*

So, go through and decide, from your point of view, if these questions are helpful or not.

Actually, this was kind of a trick question. You see, these could easily be questions you may ask yourself. They are not inherently helpful or harmful. It all depends on what you do with them. Each one has potential to help you.

For example:

You may have decided, *What did I do that was so bad to deserve this happening to me?* is a harmful question. It certainly seems like it. And it easily could be if you can't let it go and consequently start to blame yourself for being *bad*. However, it could easily be a question that can lead to spiritual growth. It may entice you to examine it, to come to your own conclusions that accidents happen, that illnesses happen, and nothing you did caused it.

This question may instill in you a desire to see what other people have said about it. To learn and then to explore your own inner feelings, gradually leading to being quite good at self-reflection and learning to form your own beliefs; beliefs that belong to you.

Or take a question that at first glance appears positive and helpful. *What lessons have I learned from my child?* Sure, sounds positive, and in my case it really was. I decided to live my life according to the way she was living hers and had demonstrated every day while she was here.

It all depends though on where you go with it. Someone could just as easily tell themselves; my child was so wonderful and he still died. Why should I even bother anymore? What's the point? Especially, if these thoughts are recurring, like a broken record, depression and hopelessness may be coming on strong. And if one doesn't seek out knowledge and try to learn as much as possible, one can get stuck and not recover.

The ability to deal with these never-ending questions relies in large part on what you can learn on your own. It's like reframing your thoughts after doing much self-reflection and all the *re's* we have talked about in earlier chapters. All this will culminate into your own *knowing* what is *your* truth, your true beliefs. Once you have identified your own truths, the path will be easier.

In my case, as I have mentioned previously, I went on a quest for knowledge before I could be even close to defining my beliefs for sure. And I got a lot of validation. I am completely comfortable with my beliefs right now, and they have eased my heart and soul. As you know, I read over two hundred books, explored research and articles on the internet, talked to countless people, paid attention to the spiritual experiences I was having, and always, always remained open-minded. This is the definition of a spiritual journey.

One of the first books I read was *Man's Search for Meaning* by Viktor E. Frankl. His experience in concentration camps where prisoners lived in bestial conditions, seemingly without hope, led him to conclusions which have helped others. With the exception of his sister, he lost his entire family in these camps.

His father, mother, brother, and his wife died in the camps or in the gas ovens there. He developed a form of therapy to help others directly face suffering and the forces of evil to transcend such a predicament and discover a truth that can save them. Frankl believed that even under the most extreme and miserable conditions, that life holds potential meaning.

Some of the many books I read that were instrumental in this spiritual journey are listed at the end of this book. *I encourage you to give them a try.*

Being *deeply loved*
by someone gives
you STRENGTH,
while *loving*
someone deeply
gives you
COURAGE.

– LAO TZU

CHAPTER EIGHT

The Survival of the Soul

25 Years in the After

Over the years, I have written articles and speeches in an effort to help others who are experiencing grief, especially the loss of a child. As a professional psychologist, I also wanted to help other professionals understand what helps, as well as what doesn't help, when they attempt to assist those experiencing a profound loss.

One of my first articles, "A Grief Shared," was written five years after Maria-Victoria died, just shortly after 9/11. I wrote others at different time intervals, with varying purposes. The last was after eighteen years.

Today, I am writing after twenty-five years of living this life. My purpose is to try to put into words what those twenty-five years have done to me, my relationships with others, and to describe what it feels like to live with this profound grief; how

I have changed. There is no doubt that such a loss affects the soul, the mind, one's sense of self, and belief systems; including evaluation of what is important in this world, and what is not important.

I believe this will resonate with many, but not with all, since we each find different ways to live the years in the *After*. Those who have experienced such profound loss know that there is now division in their life—*the Before and the After.*

So, what does it feel like after all this time? I must first tell you that it has gone very quickly, and that was a surprise, because initially I thought, "How can I live without my daughter?" "How can I live without our future together?"

I wanted to be with her, but I didn't want to leave my son or be the cause of grief to anyone. Previously in this book, I have described what earlier grief/loss feels like, so I won't repeat that. But the long-term grief, that which changes your body, mind, and soul—is different. It is very hard to find a metaphor to express this accumulation of years of grief, but one is really needed.

The Little Red and White Tugboat

THE BEFORE.

There once was a little tugboat, who thought of herself as mighty and strong, painted in pleasing colors of red and white. She was proud that she had a big responsibility in the harbor making sure that other boats were safe and could move and navigate with ease. Her steering wheel was her confidence and sense of self, her compass kept her on the right path, morally, spiritually and in relation to other boats. The engine was her brain and relied upon fuel and proper care to continue to function as a brain should. The Little Tugboat's anchor was a weight that could hold her steady but could also send her adrift if not properly maneuvered. The most important part of the little tugboat was her cabin home where her children thrived, and with wide eyes, were learning all they could about navigating the seas of life. This was the heart and soul of the tugboat, the very reason for living.

One day just after the little tug had finished pulling a large ship through the harbor, the Earth quaked, and an enormous wave came crashing totally destroying the part of the cabin where her daughter was. This was the beginning of the second part of the tugboat's life.

THE AFTER.

At the beginning of the *After*, all normal functioning parts of the tugboat are affected. The steering wheel no longer works properly; the compass is out of whack—constantly searching for some kind of equilibrium. The anchor cannot be found, the engine is so damaged it cannot produce any power, and there is no fuel.

The heart and soul of our tugboat self will sometimes seem destroyed and will always be permanently altered. However, the heart and soul can also grow.

For the first five years in the *After*, one experiences the enormity of the catastrophe. It is so hard at this time. As thoughts of such despair pull you down to where you don't want to go, one simply tries to live. The anchor has landed directly on your chest and that weight will never leave you, even after twenty-five years, although, it is much lighter now.

Other anchors have emerged to steady your boat body to keep you upright and seaworthy. These have been accompanied by lifesavers of various kinds.

One anchor for me was *Compassionate Friends,* a group dedicated to helping parents who have lost a child. Specific personal friends were also life savers. These were friends who could get over their own discomfort and fears and talk to me about my daughter. They realized that talking about her, just hearing her name, Maria-Victoria, was, and still is, like the sun shining brightly on the Earth. There will not be a lot of these friends, but one or two can be true life savers in the *After*.

Perhaps, the biggest combination anchor/life saver for me, was recognizing the value and importance of *reframing*. Making a conscious decision about my relationship with my daughter. It may have been easier for me to do this since I am a psychologist and much therapy is based upon this principle. However, learning to do it for myself was different; in the face of such hurt and pain, it requires determination.

I read hundreds of books on death and dying, the afterlife, spiritual connection, communication with those who passed, and the various different religious views about what happens to us after we die. This was combined with my own religious views and upbringing as a Methodist and Episcopalian. Added to all of this was my own scientific inclination, including studies of the survival of consciousness, theoretical links of science, and spirituality.

I needed to do this—it's a part of who I am. It may come to others more easily and quickly, or it may take more time. That's okay. The process is important and absolutely necessary for reframing.

The process requires you to *let go* of those thoughts that can pull you down to feelings of despair, depression, and hopelessness. You need to *reframe* your feelings of *why me?* as well as the anger you will most surely experience, that the most important thing in your life has been taken from you; and the complete despair of "losing connection" with, for me, my daughter.

I needed to reframe to something that could actually bring hope and the ability to live, and so do you. No one can do this for you; it is something you must do for yourself, and it must be *authentic—true to your beliefs.*

Through all my studying and reading, my reframing went something like this:

The First Stage

I had to go within myself and examine my *beliefs*.

- *I believe* that my daughter and I knew and loved each other even before we were born. We were in a dimension I would call the universe of love. She chose to be my daughter, and I chose to be her mother. We came here for experiences to broaden and strengthen our souls. Her soul was more developed than mine, so she needed less time.

- *I believe* that love is forever, and never dies. It is the substance of our surviving consciousness after death. Basically, love is all there is, and the meaning of life is to recognize that.

- *I believe* that our loved ones who have died are always there for us, and around us, but in a manner our minds cannot as yet discern.

- *I believe* that we can sometimes communicate, through love, with one another. In fact, *I know this to be true.*

- *I believe* that we will be together again, after I die, in a similar but more evolved manner as we were before our births here.

This conscious reframing is instrumental in helping one live with such devastating loss. *Reframing and delineating your own beliefs* are life-affirming. People can reframe in different ways, *but* it must be consistent with their own beliefs.

The Second Stage

The second stage of the reframing is to *redefine* your relationship with your child, or other lost loved one.

Even though you can't have a physical relationship, you can have a belief confirming connection with your child. You need to do it in your way. In my case, I honor that my daughter is with me still. Her pictures are everywhere, I talk to her most every day—sometimes several times—and I have mementoes and reminders of her scattered around my house. I keep our relationship *alive.* I cherish the memory of times when I know we have communicated more dramatically. I have told her that I physically kiss her every time I snuggle with my dog, Bailey. I can look at a specific picture and feel her essence as we hug and hold one another and give each other the pretend nose-kisses that we physically used to do all the time. We all handle grief in

different ways, but I can't imagine it any differently for me.

In our *After* redefinition of our relationship, I made a commitment to Maria-Victoria to live the rest of my life the way I thought she would have lived hers. It is one of the reasons I write and take opportunities to speak with others who have suffered loss.

My entire life has been dedicated to helping others, but I think I have become a kinder and more compassionate person over time. I am trying to catch up to the spiritual development of my daughter.

Time is another factor that is interesting. These twenty-five years have pretty much flown by, so quick it seems unbelievable. I also believe that time, being a human concoction, is simply inconsequential in the universal world. This twenty-five years is just a blip, a minute in "time."

As I have said before, I no longer have any fear of death; it is the door to where my daughter is.

I don't want to give you the impression that it is all good by doing things like reframing, redefining your relationship, and delineating your own belief system. It is not.

First, it is hard, hard work. What you find at twenty-five years in the *After*, is that you can learn to refocus when you are overwhelmed with the thoughts of horror that still strike you with recognition of what has happened. That she is really gone, or when memories of that day start to bring you to where you don't want to be. It is similar to PTSD seen in soldiers who have experienced war trauma.

For me, it is the visual memory of my beautiful daughter, looking undisturbed and peaceful, lying on a stretcher/bed within the emergency room. As I cradle her face, a warm stream of blood trickles from her mouth onto my hand.

With our little tugboat, it is like a lightning bolt has hit you, and you know if you don't do something, the entire boat will sink under the sea into the blackness—not necessarily to die, but to have all breath and life sucked out of it.

When this happens, I have learned to stop it, and quickly. I have learned to "let it go." I say to myself, sometimes out loud, "don't go there," and I refocus on something more positive.

There are a lot of *re-s* in this way of life: Re-framing, re-defining, reexamining, your personal belief system, re-focusing thoughts that can take you where you don't want to be.

But these can also help you to a path where you can *renew* your soul and keep the heart of your tugboat satisfied that love is forever.

The Christmas before my daughter died, I read a book to my children, something we did all the time. The book was called *The Christmas Box,* by Richard Paul Evans.

A main component of the story was an older widow and mother who had lost her child and invited a young couple to live in her very large house. I have not had the courage to read it again, but I did keep it. I had premonitions that something was going to happen to someone in my family especially one of my children in the months that followed this Christmas, and my daughter had some experiences as well. I have decided to close this piece by reading this little book again and then telling you how I feel afterward.

Well, I finished it, and I will admit that I cried quite a bit at the end. It certainly wasn't as hard as I imagined it would be after these twenty-five years. A question that was often posed by the older widow to the young man in the story centered on:

Do you know what the first Christmas gift was?

He could not really answer this question until near the end of the story. Two quotes from letters that the widow had written to her child are especially pertinent to end this writing.

"My beloved one,

Another Christmas season has come. The time of joy and peace. Yet how great a void still remains in my heart. They say that time heals all wounds. But even as wounds heal they leave scars, token reminders of the pain. Remember me, my love. Remember my love.

How I wish that I might say these things to your gentle face and that this box might be found empty. With Christmas—we know there is hope, my love. Hope of embracing you again and holding you to my breast. This because of the great gift of Christmas. The first Christmas offering from a parent to His children, because he loved them and wanted them back. I understand that in ways I never understood before, as my love for you has not waned with time but has grown brighter with each Christmas season. How I look forward to that glorious day that I hold you again. I love you, my little angel.'

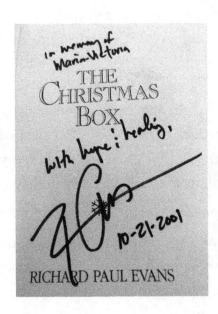

I had forgotten until I opened the first page of this book again, that it had been autographed by the author at the dedication to a beautiful angel statue in Atlanta, Georgia. It was surrounded by engraved bricks honoring children who had died. Maria-Victoria has a brick there that says: *Love and Joy.*

So now you know what the first gift of Christmas was. *Love. For me, it is love <u>and</u> hope.*

The SPIRITUAL JOURNEY is the unlearning of fear and prejudices and the *acceptance of love* back in our hearts. Love is the *essential reality* and our purpose on earth. To be *consciously aware* of it, to EXPERIENCE LOVE in ourselves and others, is the MEANING OF LIFE.

– MARIANNE WILLIAMSON

CHAPTER NINE

The Latest Chapter —
But Not the Last

Journal Entries

One of the most valuable recommendations I can make to anyone who experiences a loss is to *write it down*. Journaling is a gift to yourself that can span not only time but the depths of your soul, the universe of your emotions. It has the potential to allow you to know yourself, to look back and actually *feel* events from the past, to re-experience states of wonder, and to clarify what you know to be true. Aside from the support we receive from others, it is probably the most powerful way of coping with and understanding your own grief.

In view of my profession, I also know a lot about memory, notably its limitations and ways to enhance it. We forget an awful lot during our lives; actually, we must, since our brains cannot handle retaining all that information. But there are things we simply don't want to forget, memories that carry the gift of bringing us joy and keeping our loved ones close. To enhance the retrieval of memories, we must do something intentionally to retain them. Writing or journaling them is one such method that will ensure their survival. When you reread something that you have written in a journal, you relive it. You can see yourself doing it and experience the sensory input that accompanies it.

Journaling was very important for this book. This chapter will follow one of this book's overall purposes, so you can see some entries spanning from the very first year in the *After* to the present time. It's a little window into the various types of journaling that can bring you both peace and clarity as well as understanding of yourself and what is important to you. In my case, it is also a miniature record of travels on my spiritual journey over the course of decades of time.

1997 — The First Year

One thing I recommend that those who have suffered a profound loss, particularly the loss of a child, is to write a list of memories. I did this shortly after Maria-Victoria died because I wanted words and everyday memories that may not have been captured with a photograph. It is these everyday memories that illustrate the love in our life and are treasured beyond time and words. Reading the words brings up pictures in the mind. I can revisit these at any time and have pages and pages of such memories to comfort me. They are short and sweet and so much better than photos. Just to give you an example, here are some from my journal:

- Getting Maria-Victoria a blue ice cream cone at Baskin-Robbins and seeing her mouth turn blue.

- Making Maria-Victoria baloney and mayonnaise sand-wiches—mayonnaise must be on both slices of bread.

- Holding her hand while riding in the car.

- Going to the Powers Crossroads Fair; walking with her and picking out things.

- Maria-Victoria fixing us breakfast in bed and coming in as a waitress to take our order.

- Going to *Phantom of the Opera* at the Fox Theater.

- Watching *Wishbone* on TV together.

- Playing in the snow when we had the big snowfall.

- Riding home in the car from Boca with you lying in my arms.

- Going to *Beauty and the Beast* with Maria-Victoria, and her delight when I bought her the lighted torch.

- Singing Christmas carols on Maria-Victoria's bed on Christmas Eve, especially "What Child Is This."

- Eating crabs at Granddad's.

- Making lemon sugar cookies.

- Dressing you up as an M&M bag for Halloween.

- Coming into bed and snuggling with me in the morning.

- When you had the job of distributing all the mail.

- Seeing your face when you got your bouquets after the *Secret Garden* and the two little girls who asked for your autograph.

- When you made your famous cream cheese and jelly sandwiches.

- The first time you would sing to me and made me put my head in the pillow so I couldn't see you.

- Saying, *love you so much Mommy*.

- Your first slumber party for your birthday and David was the only boy.

- Helping you put on your makeup when you were the Koala bear in *Odyssey of the Mind*.

- The time you cut the grass for Mommy but forgot to put the power drive on and got so exhausted.

- When we had that great big black-and-white whale in Orlando and carried it to the pool.

- You, telling me how the Goldfish turned your teeth orange just after you got your braces.

- When you would get so happy when I'd get you a *prize* at the grocery store, and you would try to make a deal to get two or three.

- When you did your little old lady voice—you were so good.

- When you would play dress-up with the clothes in Mommy's closet and model for me. You looked so sophisticated.

- Watching you at ballet and tap class.

- Playing tennis together on the driveway.

- The way you laid at the foot of my bed and propped your feet up to watch TV.

- How you loved it if I'd fix you something to eat and brought it there, and you'd say, *I love you Mommy— You're the best Mommy!*

- The time we took the *Owly* blanket and laid down on the driveway together to look at the stars

And Pages and Pages More...

JOURNAL ENTRY: Nineteen Months in the After

May 12, 1998 – Our Journal

I've Come a Long Way

My Maria-Victoria,

I love you. Do you ever get tired of me saying that? That's our little joke, honey. I can't believe it's been this long, pumpkin. The pain is still here. It just doesn't go away. I guess it never will. This has been a helpful evening with me surfing the net getting good stuff about where you are. I think it's time to add this to our communication ways. I love memories, honey, especially when I can picture your *feel* in my head. I have these seconds of joy. My little seconds of joy that keep me going. I need to be close to you. And I'm having a hard time finding the right way. I feel like I can hear your little voice saying, *Mommy, you can't work so much.* I need time to be with my little one, just like I needed time when you were physically here. I guess I need to search for the ways to be true to you and me. I think tomorrow I'll talk to you on the way to work. I think I have been numbing myself lately, and that's not good. I so want to feel you and know you're around. Let's see how you can show me you're around. Sweet dreams to me and kisses, kisses to you. Mommy loves you.

From near the beginning of the After until now. What a spiritual journey we have been on my love.

JOURNAL ENTRY: 4 ½ Years in the After

March 3, 2001

When I decided to write today, I picked up this journal I haven't looked at for quite some time. So much has happened to me and my family since I wrote these words. But it's appropriate that I am writing in this particular journal since it started out as a book about happiness and its pursuit and special moments of happiness.

I'm not sure I'm even pursuing happiness anymore. Obviously, this is a pretty down day, but there is still hope in my soul. Hope is the life preserver of the soul. I have learned this in these years that have been filled with so much pain and deadened attempts at any semblance of happiness. I have commented before that going through all this pain of losing Maria-Victoria has made me a better person, but has it really? I don't really know. I feel I put such expectations on myself that I should be so good at dealing with everything that I don't let myself be truly vulnerable.

Yesterday, when I learned about a terrible remark that had been made about a member of my family, I felt such hurt and anger that I seldom ever "allowed" me to feel. Hurt and anger are so closely tied, and I found myself vacillating back and forth from one to the other, but it became a catalyst for the need to write these words, and a catalyst to look at my life and this whole concept of happiness.

I question whether happiness, true happiness (whatever that is) and joy will ever be possible for me. I felt joy was totally gone from my life when Maria-Victoria died, but to live without any semblance of joy is simply to exist. I want to do more than just exist. How do I bring joy back into my life?

What do I know about myself right now? I know my children are part of my being, a part of my soul. When I physically lost Maria-Victoria, I lost a big part of myself, a part of my soul. David is a part of my being, a part of my soul. If he is hurt, I am hurt. If he is disparaged, I am disparaged. If he is loved, I am loved. If he is happy, I am happy. If he is content, I am content. This I know. Maria-Victoria must fill up the space in my spiritual soul. If she is remembered, our love is remembered.

What else do I know about myself? I need to be brutally honest. Probably like everyone I'm basically selfish. I like time to myself. I like to write but don't give myself the gift of doing so as I should. Just like today, this writing is a gift to myself. Since Maria-Victoria died, I've often felt a frenetic need to make things right. As if I had such power! I can't make things right—I'll never be able to do that.

What else do I know about me? I enjoy gaining knowledge in my field and being productive. I like to have knowledge so I can teach others, but now I want to be in control and do only what I want to do. I don't want people putting extra burdens on me or expect me to solve problems I have no interest in solving. I want to control where I put my energy.

I want close friendships and intimacy, but I need to keep some distance. I enjoy sharing, relating to others, and feeling special bonds, but I get bored pretty quickly if something is not of mutual interest.

I love beauty and seeing beautiful things around me. I want surroundings that provide pleasure to the eye, in terms of color, contour, brightness. I love my home and want it filled with symbols of love and beauty. I am drawn to both Victorian images and classical looks as well as more simplistic shapes and contours with bright and bold contrasting colors. This is a part of me. I like the design aspect—it's fun (what is fun?—something to address later). Sometimes I go overboard and make mistakes—but that's okay.

I feel deeply for people and have a strong need to ease their pain, which is often translated into "fixing their problem." I have to watch this because it's never possible, and to take on such a burden is too heavy.

I am basically an optimist, though more pessimism has made its way into my life over the last five years. I expect people to do the right thing, to be kind, helpful, encouraging and when they are not, I am quick to become angry and want to write them off. I have become much more tolerant of the little things, but I am quick to anger at what I view as major assaults. I'm hurt more deeply by this because I expect people to be better than they are. And when they show that they are not, I take and feel it personally.

Oprah does a segment sometimes called—*What I know for sure.*

Things I know for sure:

- There is no greater love than that of mother and child.

- I would fight to the death to protect my children.

- Actions based on the intent of love and compassion bring love and compassion back to you.

- You never really know what's going on with a person.

- I love my dog.

- You never really know how other people view you. You may be pleasantly or unpleasantly surprised.

- The only thing that matters is how you feel about yourself.

- Relationships are always good and bad, positive and negative. Cherish the positive, nurture it. Deal with the negative; don't let negative thoughts fester.

- Let other people know about their own goodness.

- Forgive yourself for both real and imagined transgressions.

- Be passionate about what you truly believe.

- If you are not true to yourself, you will never be happy.

- Happiness is in giving. Let others give to you, so they can be happy too.

- Let go of the outcome.

- When I have been hurt by a person, my first response (after anger and fleeting thoughts of revenge), is to cut them off—to distance myself from them. I think you must give it some time and then decide if any action is worth taking, whether it's viewed as positive or negative. The key is whether you are being true to yourself. Any action, when you are true to yourself, is correct.

These journal entries, you will probably see immediately, are more unusual. Let me explain. Especially in the early years. My daughter and I would communicate where I would ask her a question, wait for a response, and then write it down. It was that simple. Before doing this, I would usually meditate, as deeply as possible, always in a peaceful environment.

These are actual communications I had with my daughter:

August 30, 2000

It's the age-old question in our personal journey sweet-heart—how do we communicate; how do we share our love in this new circumstance? I so want to talk to you—to share feelings. Sometimes I think I've accepted that our physical relationship is gone, but I know our spiritual relationship can be stronger. I just know.

I'm going to ask you a question and listen for your answer. We did this before, remember—but I've gotten lazy—or scared—or depressed or something. Meditation really helps though. Deep meditation.

So, here's a question for today:

Our love is so strong—how do I give my love to you now?
Answer: In Joy Enjoy. FLY – Soar with Purpose

What do you enjoy most about your new life?
Answer: Music—tinkling of bells, Animals, Swirls, Dance—*Mom, it's so cool!*

November 2, 2000

What was it like for you right after the accident? Were you afraid? Did others help you?

Answer: You breathe into a newness. It just is.

Do you get mad at me when I cry?

Answer: Tears nourish the soul.

January 30, 2002

What can I do that will bring you joy?

Answer: Love what you do, do what you love.

Throughout this journey, I have often talked with my daughter in this way. It requires much quiet, a calming of the body and soul, and attention and listening. Meditation is particularly helpful. In most cases, the "answers" do not reflect the way I would say something, but to me are more profound. It brings me close to Maria-Victoria, as well as giving me insight.

February 25, 2023

I can't believe I am actually getting close to finishing *The Book*. Although my spiritual journey is still on-going, I can reflect on both where I am now and how astounding this journey has been. I am enthusiastic about future travels and what I will learn from them, how I will be impacted and how I may be able to help others examine their own spiritual growth over time.

We are all individuals molded by our life experiences, our upbringing, by variables such as where we were born, the family we were born into, the resources we had or didn't have, our schooling, our genetics—so much—so very much—left up to variables. I have been awed to realize how many people have been instrumental in affecting how I have come to be the person I am now. It is also rather awe-inspiring to reflect upon all those people who have been a part of my life and their contributions (both positive and negative) to my spiritual development and the comfort I feel from my state of spirituality right now. This spiritual journey is the epitome of educational achievement because it is a learning experience, with no degrees given, but reflects the internal calm that comes from being a *lifetime learner,* a favorite expression of my best friend.

We should never, ever stop learning. We learn not only from the positive experiences in our lives but from the many negative things that will happen to all of us. I do believe that self-understanding is a very valuable commodity especially if accompanied by both *self-forgiveness* and *the ability to forgive others*. You can forgive and still remember. In fact, you need to remember, so you can use it to guide your future life. But forgiving and then letting go frees your soul.

When I was a child, I went to church and Sunday school as a Methodist, and my grandmother was the one who really taught me all the stories from the Bible. I am very thankful for that. Over all these years, I have had a metamorphosis in my thoughts and beliefs about what it all means and what I believe now. This growth has continued and still evolves as each new day passes. Much has changed for me in the past couple of years, more so than it did for decades. I have always believed in God, and I have always believed in the teachings of Jesus, because they reflect love and I know that God is Love. I recognize that part of the reason I believe in this is the *variable* of the family I was born into. However, more than most people, I have had life experiences that made me read, study, and explore all I could find to understand spirituality in all its forms and respect all points of view, all true religious and spiritual beliefs.

I know what I don't believe—extremism in any religion, including Christianity. In my office waiting room I have a framed plaque that illustrates that basically all the major religions in the world share the Christian saying, *Do unto others as you would have them do unto you.* This plaque includes the same sentiment in Buddhism, Judaism, Hinduism, Islam, and Native American.

I strongly feel that true spirituality or any religion should not be based on fear or punishment or *rules* that could reflect what the previous environment may have been like ages ago and a desire to use *religion* to make laws, especially to denigrate or exclude people. That makes no sense to me. Rather, for me, it is all about love. Remember God is Love. Love Never Dies and Love Is All There Is.

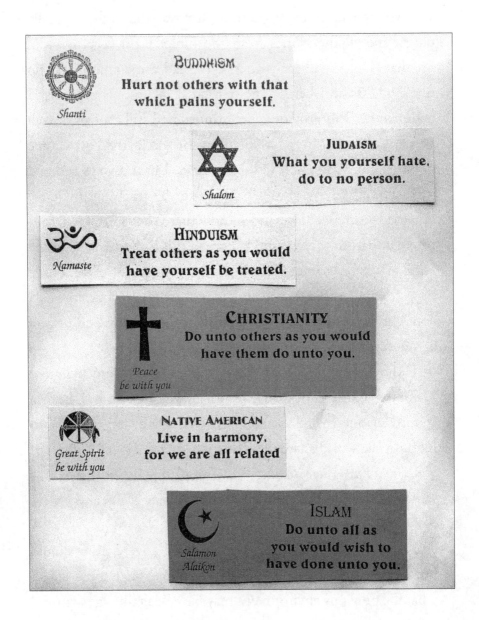

I write all of this to make it clear that I believe that the universe is too complex, too wondrous to not have a universal intelligence behind it, a universal consciousness, so much greater than just mere mortals; more than we could ever imagine or put into words. In other words, God. My God is a loving and accepting God, not a fearful one. This belief is not in conflict with science, not in the least. Much work is being done in this area, merging science, spirituality, quantum physics, and scientific understanding of synchronicities (coincidences), that may reflect God's hand is in it all.

Over the past few years, my mind has opened up further to try to understand others' points of view and the variety of religious and spiritual beliefs others may have. (This is a part of the journey and an important one.) I would much rather look at how we are *alike* than how we are different. I would rather emphasize what we *should* do, not what we shouldn't do. I want to emphasize doing what is right, simply because it is the right thing to do. Living like this will bring you peace. Loving like this will bring you joy.

At this point in this incredible personal spiritual journey, I can say unequivocally that…

I am happy.

*True, real love expands your soul,
not just your heart and mind.*

I have found joy again.

I have let myself be vulnerable.

I am and will always be true to myself.

I never want to hurt anyone.

Kindness is a guiding principle in my life.

I vow to always have an open mind.

Magical, mystical moments* are a gift from God.

God is in charge.

I am here to learn.

I will never stop learning.

I am fulfilling my purpose for being here.

*All of the truly deep loves we have been given
on this Earth, are gifts from God beyond measure.
And these deep loves will be with us eternally.*

It feels good to be taken care of.

I am more alive now than I ever have been.

I love my dog.

*Thank you, Lee Marvin

We *think*
we listen, but
very rarely do
we listen with *real*
understanding,
real empathy.
Yet LISTENING,
of this special kind,
is one of the *most potent*
forces for change
that I know.

– CARL ROGERS

Epilogue

In many ways, the writing of this book has been like a *life review*. Those of you who are familiar with near-death experiences, know that it is often a part of that.

I started studying near-death experiences before David or Maria-Victoria were even born. I am indebted to Dr. Raymond Moody, the author of *Life After Life*, one of the most important books I have ever read. I had the pleasure of meeting and talking with him on two occasions, and I consider him an instrumental part of my spiritual journey. Dr. Moody is the one who coined the term *near-death experiences or NDE's*.

At the time, I was enrolled in a *Death and Dying* course in graduate school. By coincidence, my mom was dying of cancer at age fifty. In many ways, Dr. Moody's work was a true beginning of the merging of science and spirituality—at least for me. Many subsequent books and articles on NDE's were written by physicians who were in the position of actually witnessing these happening. They interviewed their surviving patients, who reported floating up to the ceiling or beyond, and then describing exactly what each professional did and said while they were clinically dead.

Some could describe again from an out of body and up in the air vantage point things there is no explanation for. For example, I remember reading about a woman who had clinically died and reported that she saw a red shoe on the roof of the hospital during the experience. This was later confirmed when the shoe was recovered from the roof. There is a plethora of work that has been done on near-death experiences and knowledge of these types of *evidences* of hope, can be very comforting to those who have lost loved ones.

One of the things often experienced is a *life review* but not exactly what you may be expecting. Rather than just reviewing events during your life and interactions with others, the person having the NDE would report that they *felt the feelings* of the person(s) they were interacting with during their review. Or, in other words—how others felt and responded to you throughout your life. Quite a sobering thought. It made a big impression on me.

With this *life review* of my own, I have come to several important revelations and understandings. The first of these is that *there are so many good people in this world.*

In today's atmosphere of discord, often an *us vs them* mindset, rather nasty political and even religious intolerance, and constant opinionated people berating others, one can easily forget or overlook that. Discord is the product of this kind of world turmoil.

However, if we can get beyond that and really see people for who they are, it is amazing how good, kind, helpful, and compassionate so many people are. I really notice that every day now. My eyes were truly opened to this during this life review, and I am grateful for all these good people in the world.

Another major revelation involved the number of *lessons* we have the opportunity to learn by living a life here. Maybe I can talk about a few—since there are so many and I am willing to bet they are all important—whether it's to you or me.

For some of us, it may take a very long time to learn them— or to communicate them if that is part of our purpose. We may grow to be quite old, and some would label it *wisdom.* Others, like my daughter, don't need as much time. They are already wise in knowing what is really important in this world.

Surely one of my life lessons is the appreciation of the value of kindness. You know I always knew that Maria-Victoria was kind and cared about others, but I don't think I realized the depth and naturalness of that kindness until I read those letters written by her classmates. The naturalness of being a kind soul—someone who first thinks about the other person, rather than themselves, is something to strive for. It has taken me an entire longer life to really understand that "naturalness of kindness" and why it is so priceless. When you don't even have to think about it, and it just comes naturally, should be everybody's goal.

Another lesson that means so much to me is the value of true connection. Sometimes you have to be brave to reach out and seek that deeper connection with another human being (or spiritual being). You are taking a chance and we all know how scary that can be! Many may never get there—being afraid to take the plunge. However, courage can really pay off as the depth of understanding of another person helps you to better understand yourself.

I have learned to have true connection both in this world on Earth, and across dimensions. I can't even put into words what that means to me. Perhaps the best word is *love*. That depth of connection is kind of what love is all about.

That level of connection with my daughter allowed me to have an experience that is simply too wondrous to describe. Some may call it a dream—but I don't. When you have experienced something that miraculous, it simply doesn't matter what anyone else wants to call it. Although I may have been technically asleep (and alive), I ascended with my daughter into her realm—what some would call heaven. I will never forget this, the feeling—that incredible feeling. We rose upward together— through beauty and light with such monumental feelings of peace and of love dispersing through our entire beings. It was joy and pure acceptance. I was out of my body and it didn't matter—we were merging in spirit. I am thankful for that experience—whatever it was. And it is one of those experiences where I don't have to prove it to anybody.

I think I mentioned I had an overwhelming feeling of peace and blessing at the very moment when I was holding my daughter's face in my hands after the accident, as she lay on the bed in the emergency room, when I was finally able to see her. Right after feeling her warm blood from her mouth on my hand, I was enveloped in a feeling of peace and pure love as if I was being told everything is all right. I didn't cry—I was being comforted by something much greater than I could ever imagine. This truly seems like the ultimate in connection.

Another life lesson that is very important to me is the value of knowledge. I am still learning and will be until the day I die—or perhaps even after. It could be that we will you know, and *probably knowledge acquisition continues in the heaven dimension.* It is amazing what you can learn throughout your life. I feel I learn something new every day or at least expand on something I have already learned. I most certainly have learned what is important and what is not important. I have also learned to *let go.* We have to realize when we have done all we can do; when it is time to go on to different adventures and priorities in our lives. You realize that things you may have viewed as very important in your youth are simply inconsequential now. In a reverse mode, you decide to prioritize those things you may have neglected and make them paramount in your life. And it all has to do with knowledge—especially self-knowledge. It is a way of investing in yourself.

One of the more recent developments in my spiritual journey that has been pivotal for me is to allow myself to be vulnerable. Many folks would not feel that this is a big deal—but for someone like me, it truly is. I have lived most of my life with a self-imposed protective suit of armor. Before Maria-Victoria died, and even when I was a little girl, I had this protective suit of heavy-duty fabric around me—a way to fend off any assaults suggesting I couldn't handle things on my own or to fight off potential criticisms from others. From my earliest years, I felt a heavy sense of responsibility and the need to help others—frequently to rescue them. Although that sounds like a good thing to most people, it certainly has its downsides. Over the years, that heavy-duty fabric turned into a very strong suit of armor that protected me from having to show any vulnerability, at least in public. I was kind of known as a *warrior* for principles and integrity, and people knew I would fight for things I believed were right. I don't regret that warrior mentality at all, but I have come to recognize that not allowing myself to be vulnerable likely affected me emotionally.

So, when I began to let that go, to let those emotions seep out through the armor, I realized how easily I could be hurt, and how easily I can cry. And I realized that it is okay to show that side of me to others who truly care about me. Big revelation! And after all these years. Sometimes you just have to *not be the one who is always strong*. It is okay for someone else to take care of you. Letting people help you, watch out for you, allows them to show *their goodness*. So, I advise parents who are going through such a tremendous loss not to be afraid to show your vulnerability and to accept care from others.

After all, that is what love is.

A Final Thought About Love

Much of this story has been about love. Love is so important for your soul, in fact, it is the reason for your existence on this Earth. To feel love, to give love, to feel the 'exquisiteness' of true love as it embraces your heart and soul.

A letter written to my daughter shortly after she died.

My dearest daughter,

I remember your saying to me so many times, "Mommy, do you ever get tired of me saying 'I love you' so much?" My heart would just swell and I would tell you I could never get tired of hearing those wonderful words. Now, when I say to you over and over again in my thoughts and whispers, 'I love you'—I wonder—do you ever get tired of me saying that?

I cannot stop saying it because I so want you to know. That must have been the same for you. What a love we have! It is such a beautiful, indescribable love. How do you put in words feelings beyond our own understanding. I love all the things about you and most of all I love the "you" of you.

Whenever I looked into your eyes or looked at your face, I felt such immense love and awe that I had you to love. You sent love to me always. I treasured that you could love me so – that I had been given such a gift to my soul.

I loved every nuance of you. I loved it when you first woke up in the morning, you would come looking for me, wanting to be held and caressed and comforted. We would cling to one another for a long time, kiss and rub noses—sometimes be silly. We both delighted in the expression of our love.

I loved watching your face. Do you remember sometimes you would ask me what I was doing when I was looking at you so intensely? Well, I was looking at you with awe that you were a part of me. My eyes would caress your most beautiful eyes, your skin so pure and luminous, your nose—straight and proud. I loved your eyebrows; they were so perfectly arched—I loved to trace them with my finger. I especially loved this sitting by your bed, before you went to sleep at night – feeling the joy of such exquisite love.

You were so cuddly. Remember how you always wanted to cuddle – and I did too. It felt so good to hold you. When we held or hugged, we fit together so well, and it was pure joy to snuggle under a blanket and be together. There was much more than physical closeness. I felt we were sharing the same space—our energy was merged together and that was the way it was supposed to be.

I loved all your little ways. The way you would shift from 'my little girl' to a 'woman of the world', sometimes in a flash. I love each one because they each were delightful. I loved when you would dress up in my clothes and create outfits and then give a fashion show for me and Tom. I loved it when you washed your hair and put on your big white robe and would sit in front of me while I dried your hair and brushed it. I loved when you put make-up on and you would come out to me to show me your look. Sometimes I would be in awe that you were growing up, but most of the time I was just enthralled with your beauty. I loved it when you would come home after school and plop down in front of the TV in my bedroom – in your special position. I loved making you a snack or macaroni and cheese and hearing you say, "I love you Mommy—you're the best Mommy." You always said that whenever I did something for you or bought you a present. And sometimes, for no reason at all.

I loved your bounciness. Your excitement about doing things. You loved it when we did things together. I loved it when you made little things, like my heart, the pink pig from an egg and the felt seal puppet. I loved it when we would have negotiations about chores and jobs so you could earn money and the frustration you felt when David got to do things you wanted to do. I even loved your "pouting"—that reminded me of your 'temper tamps' when you were little where I would just hold you up and let you kick your feet and then we'd all end up laughing!

I loved your exuberance pumpkin, how you could take the ordinary and make it fun and exciting. But I also loved your quiet nature, your kindness and such caring for others. I loved the way you related to Tom—how you would get so upset with his teasing and how you eventually learned to be his match.

I especially loved that we had indeed become best friends. It was such fun to do things together—to go out to Chic-Fil-A, to go shopping at the mall and to go to our favorite antique store. There can be nothing greater in the world than the love we shared. It was, and is, so pure, so incredibly  strong, from the depths of our souls. I have known the very greatest love one soul can have for another. It will never leave me and I have been blessed with this 'knowing'.

The little words "I love you" seem so tiny in comparison to the immensity of my love for you sweetheart. But I will say them over and over again so you can collect them all and scatter them around to others not as fortunate as we, for that is your nature.

I love you my baby,
Mommy

Thank You Just Isn't Enough

There are so many people in my life that have been Anchors and Lifesavers as I have gone through this incredible spiritual journey. I am so afraid I will leave someone out, but I want to acknowledge as many of these folks as I can. They have been instrumental in helping me survive the grief and in their individual ways have been a big part of my spiritual growth.

Dr. Janice Kilburn – Don Stout – Connie Gouge – Dr. Bill Allen – Tom Whitehead – Dr. Wayne Jones – Dr. Bill Jensen – Dr. Joe Nail – Dr. David Hermann – John Edward – Dr. Gary Schwartz – Theresa Slavik – Frank (Buz) Smith – Fred Lacey – Betsy Foulk – Shelley Drummond – Abbie Huber – Martha Carroll – Andy

Ordyna-Pimental – Amy Whittaker – Barbara Hood – Beckie Morris – Freddie Saye – Charlotte Saye – Bettie Calhoun – Bob Hudak – Carol Allessio – Chris Allessio – Dr. Eric Fier – Erin Hicks – Peggy Thomas – Erskine Rogers – Eugenia Wattles – Vi Clement – The Jobe Family – Judy Carter – Marsha Hood – Tom Bruton – Kelly Dennard – Kristie Heath – Kylie Jo Hood – Libby Torbush – Mark Gillett – Matt Finn – Millie Bankston – Rebecca and Danny Bates – Ginger Sack – All My Compassionate Friends – Nellie E. Lake – Teachers, Administrators and Staff of Griffin-Spalding County School System – Teachers and Administrators of Westminster Elementary School – Teachers of ClearWater Academy – Maria-Victoria's Classmates who wrote those wonderful letters – Lenore Field – Viki and Ken Bozeman – Dr. Raymond Moody – Albert Einstein

ACKNOWLEDGMENTS

Cover Design Artist: Satori at 99designs

Cover Design Mentor at Author Ready: Kirsten Capunay

Cover Consultant: Richard Paul Evans

Content Editor: Debbie Rasmussen

Proofing and Copy Editor; ebook Interior Design: Kim Audrey

Interior Design & Layout: Francine Platt, Eden Graphics, Inc.

RECOMMENDED BOOKS AND RESOURCES

Compassionate Friends – National

A non-profit, self-help organization offering friendship, under-standing and hope to bereaved families that have experienced the death of a child. In the United States there are more than 500 chapters in all 50 states and Washington, D.C. , Puerto Rico and Guam. The National website provides support and help to find a local chapter near you. **compassionate friends.org**

We Need Not Walk Alone – We Are the Compassionate Friends

Compassionate Friends – Atlanta, Georgia, Tucker Chapter: tcfatlanta.org

Alexander, Eben, M.D. and Newell, Karen, *Living in a Mindful Universe: A Neurosurgeon's Journey into the Heart of Consciousness*, 2017

Proof of Heaven: A Neurosurgeon's Journey into the Afterlife, 2012, Simon and Schuster

Anderson, George and Barone, Andrew, *Lessons From the Light: Extraordinary Messages of Comfort and Hope from the Other Side*, 1999, G. P. Putnam's Sons

Brussat, Fredrick and MaryAnn, *Spiritual Literacy*, 1996 Scribner

Carlson, Richard Ph.D. and Shield, Benjamin Ph.D., Editors, *Handbook for the Soul,* 1995, Little, Brown and Company

Cosman, Mark, *In the Wake of Death: Surviving the Loss of a Child*, 1996, Moyer-Bell Publishing

D'Arcy, Paula, *Gift of the Red Bird: A Spiritual Encounter* –1996, Crossroad Publishers

Devers, Edia Ph.D., *Goodbye Again: Experiences with Departed Loved Ones*, 1997, Andrews and McMeel

Dubois, Allison, *Secrets of the Monarch*, 2007, Fireside Press

Eadie, Bettie J. *Embraced by the Light*, 1992, Gold Leaf Press

Edward, John, *Crossing Over, The Stories Behind the Stories*, 2001, Jodere Group Publishing
After Life: Answers From the Other Side, 2003, Hay House

Finkbeiner, Ann K. *After the Death of a Child*, 1996, The Free Press

Goodman, Sandy, *Love Never Dies: A Mother's Journey from Loss to Love*, 2001, Jodere Group

Grant, Robert J., *The Place We Call Home: Exploring the Soul's Existence after Death*, 2000, A.R.E. Press

Greyson, Bruce, M.D. *After: A Doctor Explores What Near-Death Experiences Reveal about Life and Beyond*, 2021, St. Martin's Publishing Group

Guggenheim, Bill and Judy, *Hello from Heaven: A New Field of Research, After Death Communication, Confirms that Life and Love are Eternal*, 1995, Bantam

Haberstam, Yitta and Leventhal, Judith, *Small Miracles Two: Heartwarming Gifts of Extraordinary Coincidences*, 1998, Adams Media Corp.

Hebel, Bruce Dr. and Hebel, Toni, *Forgiving Forward,* 2011, Regenerating Life Press

Hickman, Martha Whitmore, *I Will Not Leave You Desolate: Some Thoughts for Grieving Parents,* 1982, The Upper Room

Healing After Loss: Daily Meditations for Working Through Grief, 1994, Avon Books

Hillman, James, *The Soul's Code: In Search of Character and Calling,* 1996 Random House

Kubler-Ross, Elisabeth, *On Life After Death,* 1991, Celestial Arts

On Death and Dying and Dying, 1969, Scribner, 50th Anniversary Edition, 2019

The Wheel of Life: A Memoir of Living and Dying, 1997, Scribner

Kushner, Harold S., *When Bad Things Happen to Good People,* 1981, Avon Books

Who Needs God, 1989, Pocket Books

LaGrand, Louis E., Ph.D, *After Death Communication: Final Farewells—Extraordinary Experiences of Those Mourning the Death of Loved Ones,* 1998, Llewellyn Publications

Levine, Stephen, *Who Dies?: An Investigation of Conscious Living and Conscious Dying,* 1982, Anchor Books, Doubleday

Levy, Naomi, *To Begin Again: The Journey Toward Comfort, Strength, and Faith in Difficult Times* 1999, Alfred A. Knopf

Lommel, Pim Van M.D., *Consciousness Beyond Life: The Science of the Near Death Experience,* 2010 Harper One

Long, Jeffrey With Paul Perry, *Evidence of the Afterlife: The Science of Near Death Experiences,* 2009

God and the Afterlife: The Groundbreaking New Evidence for God and Near-Death Experiences 2016, Harper One

Love, Mary Kathryn, *Grace*, 1997 Hazelden

Martin, Joel and Romanowski, Patricia, *Love Beyond Life: The Healing Power of After-Death Communications,* 1997, Harper Collins Publishers

Miller, Sukie, Ph.D. With Suzanne Lipsett, *After Death: Mapping the Journey*, 1997, Simon and Schuster

Moody, Raymond A, M.D, Ph.D., *Life After Life: The Investigation of a Phenomenon, Survival of Bodily Death*, 1975, Mockingbird Books

Reflections on Life After Life, 1977, Bantam Books

With Dianne Arcangel, *Life After Loss: Conquering Grief and Finding Hope*, 2001– HarperCollins Publishing

Muller, Wayne, *How Then Shall We Live: Four Simple Questions that Reveal the Beauty and Meaning of Our Lives*, 1997, Bantam Books

Neal, Mary C. T*o Heaven and Back: A Doctor's Extraordinary Account of Heaven, Angels and Life Again, A True Story,* 2012

Newberg, Andrew M.D., D'Aquill, M.D. PhD. And Rause, Vince, *Why God Won't Go Away: Brain Science and the Biology of Belief,* 2001, Ballantine Books

Neeld, Elizabeth Harper PhD, *Seven Choices: Finding Daylight After Loss Shatters Your World*, 2003, Warner Books

Northrop, Suzane, *Second Chance: Healing Messages from the Afterlife*, 2002, Jodere Group, Inc.

Everything Happens for a Reason: Love, Free Will, and the Lessons of the Soul, 2021, 5-4-05, Jodere Group, Inc.

Nuland, Sherwin B., *How We Die*, 1993, Alfred A. Knopf, Inc.

Oslis, Karlis, Ph.D and Haraldsson, Erlendur, Ph.D, *At the Hour of Death: A New Look at Evidence for Life After Death*, Third Edition, 1977, Hastings House Publishers

Randles, Jenny and Hough, Peter, *Life After Death and the World Beyond: Investigating Heaven and the Spiritual Dimension*, 1998, Sterling Publishing Company

Renfield, James, *The Celestine Prophesy: An Adventure*, 1993, Warner Books, Inc.

and Adrienne, Carol, *The Celestine Prophecy: An Experiential Guide*, 1995, Warner Books

The Tenth Insight, 1996, Warner Books, Inc.

The Celestine Vision, 1997 Warner Books

Ritchie, George and Sherrill, Elizabeth, *Return from Tomorrow*, 2007, Chosen Books

Roberts, Jane, Seth Speaks, *The Eternal Validity of the Soul*, 1972, Amber-Allen Publishing

Rosen, Eliot Jay, *Experiencing the Soul: Before Birth, During Life, After Death*, 1998, Hay House

Sabom, Michael Dr., *Light and Death: One Doctor's Fascinating Account of Near-Death Experiences*, 1998, Zondervan Press

Schwartz, Gary E. Ph.D., *Super Synchronicity: Where Science and Spirit Meet*, 2017, Parem Media, Inc.

The Afterlife Experiments, with William L. Simon, 2002, Atria Books

The Truth About Medium, with William Simon, 2005, Hampton Roads

The G. O. D Experiments: With William Simon, How Science is Discovering God in Everything Including Us, 2006, Atria Books

Shield, Benjamin and Carlson, Richard, Editors, *For the Love of God: Handbook for the Spirit*, 1997, Publishers Group West

Steiger, Brad and Sherry Hanen Steiger, *Children of the Light: The Startling and Inspiring Truth About Children's Near Death Experiences*, 1995, Penguin Press

Steinpach, Richard Dr., *Why We Live After Death*, 1996 Grail Foundation Press

Van Praagh, James, *Talking to Heaven*, 1997, Penguin Group

Reaching to Heaven: A Spiritual Journey Through Life and Death, 1999, Penguin Group

Walsh, Neale David, *Conversations with God: Book One – An Uncommon Dialogue*, 1995, Tarcher, Periges

Conversations with God: Book Two – Living in the World with Honesty, Courage and Love, 1997/2020 Hampton Road Publishing Co.

Conversations with God: Book Three – Embracing the Love of the Universe –1998, Hampton Roads Publishing Company

Conversations with God: Book Four – Awaken the Species, A New and Unexpected Dialogue, 2017, Rainbow Ridge Books

Friendship with God: An Uncommon Dialogue, 1999, G. P. Putnam's Sons

Walsh, Roger, M.D. PhD, *Essential Spirituality*, 1999, John Wiley and Sons

Walton, Charlie, *When There are No Words: Finding Your Way to Cope with Loss and Grief*, 1996, Pathfinder Publishing

Weiss, Brian L. M.D., *Through Time Into Healing*, 1992, Simon and Schuster

Whitfield, Barbara Harris, 1998 *Final Passage,* Health Communications, Inc.

Wholey, Dennis, *When the Worst that Can Happen Already Has: Conquering Life's Most Difficult Times,* 1992, Berkley Publishing

Yancey, Philip, *Where is God When It Hurts,* 1999, Zondervan Publishing

Zelaski, Carol, *The Life of the World to Come: Near-Death Experience and Christian Hope,* 1996, Oxford University Press

Zukav, Gary, *The Dancing Wu Li Masters: An Overview of the New Physics,* 1979

Soul Stories, 2000, Simon and Schuster

and Francis, Linda, *The Heart of the Soul, Emotional Awareness,* 2001, Simon and Schuster

About the Author

LYNDA BOUCUGNANI-WHITEHEAD, PH.D

Dʀ. Lʏɴᴅᴀ (as she is known to most) lives in Fayetteville, Georgia, just outside of Atlanta. She is retired from her private practice as a neuropsychologist but still maintains great interest in the field. Currently, she does volunteer work in helping older individuals maintain both strong mental and physical capabilities, especially those dealing with neurological issues. She enjoys teaching classes about the brain and what others can do to enhance their memory and other functions as they age, as well as still helping parents and teachers with the issues they may be encountering with their children. Dr. Lynda maintains a comprehensive website—**drlynda.net**—which offers free information to educators and parents about numerous childhood issues, as well as dealing with grief. She continues to give speeches regarding profound grief and her contact information can be found on her website. Dr. Lynda enjoys being with her family, being a writer, photography, digital art and most especially dogs, notably beagles and basset hounds.

Printed in the USA
CPSIA information can be obtained
at www.ICGtesting.com
JSHW011357300923
49235JS00001B/3